# Wizards

# WIZARDS

## THE QUEST FOR THE WIZARD
## FROM MERLIN TO HARRY POTTER

### JOHN MATTHEWS

BARRON'S

DEDICATION

## To Gareth Knight: a modern magus

AUTHOR ACKNOWLEDGMENTS

*Thanks to my wife, Caitlín, for her generous help with research, and for her suggestions regarding some of the practical material. To my son, Emrys, for his help in researching* Star Wars. *To everyone at Godsfield Press and Bridgewater Books for their magnificent design work and support throughout this project.*

First edition for the United States and Canada published in 2003 by Barron's Educational Series, Inc.

First published in Great Britain in 2003 by Godsfield Press Ltd, Laurel House, Station Approach, Alresford, Hampshire SO24 9JH, UK. http://www.godsfieldpress.com

Designed and produced by The Bridgewater Book Company

Project Designer: John Grain
Designer: Jon Raimes
Project Editor: Nicola Wright
Picture Researcher: Vanessa Fletcher

All inquiries should be addressed to: Barron's Educational Series, Inc. 250 Wireless Boulevard Hauppauge, New York 11788 http://www.barronseduc.com

International Standard Book Number 0-7641-5637-3

Library of Congress Catalog Card Number 2002109240

Printed in China

9 8 7 6 5 4 3 2 1

PICTURE CREDITS

In instances not extensively covered by fair usage, every effort has been made to obtain permissions from holders of copyright material. If however—either through a mistake or through circumstances beyond our control—any copyright owner has been omitted, the author and publisher extend their apologies and undertake to rectify the situation in the next edition.

AKG, LONDON: p. 24 Louvre, Paris.
ART ARCHIVE: pp. 27 Bodleian Library, Oxford, 82 Dagli Orti/Cava Deitirreni Abbey, Salerno.
ATENEUM HELSINKI/THE CENTRAL ARCHIVES: pp. 71 & 73.
BRIDGEMAN ART LIBRARY, LONDON: pp. 2 Delaware Art Museum, Wilmington, 11 National Gallery of Scotland, Edinburgh, 19 Fitzwilliam Museum, University of Cambridge, 76 Stair Sainty Mattiesen Gallery, New York, 78 Birmingham Museum and Art Gallery, 81 Metropolitan Museum of Art, 85 Collection Kharbine-Tapabor, Paris, 92 Private Collection.

CAMERON COLLECTION: pp. 28, 29, 66, 67, 89, 91, 108, 116.
CORBIS: pp. 8 Ricahrd T. Nowitz, 16 Archivo Iconographico S.A./Suermondt Ludwig Museum, Aacheñ, 23 Kimbel Art Museum, 25 Mimmo Jodice, 34 Michael Freeman, 39 Bernard Annebicque/Sygma, 53 Aaron Horowitz, 63 John M. Roberts, 65 Hulton-Deutsch, 69 & 70 Bettmann, 74 Peter Wilson, 87 Archivo Iconographico S.A., 94 Hulton-Deutsch, 95 Sygma, 96 Bettmann, 100 Richard Hamilton Smith, 107 Bettmann, 113 John Paul Endress, 118 Adam Woolfitt, 120 Burstein Collection, 124 Archivo Iconographico S.A., 126 Bettmann, 138 Dave Bartruff.

COURTESY HALLS OF KING ARTHUR, TINTAGEL: p. 30.
DERBY MUSEUM & ART GALLERY: p. 102.
GETTYIMAGES/STONE: p. 99 Betsie Van der Meer.
JOHN HOWE © HARPER COLLINS: p. 12.
THE KOBAL COLLECTION: p. 64 Allarts/Camera/Cinea.
LAMBETH PALACE LIBRARY: p. 44.
ALAN LEE: p. 43.
LIBRARY OF CONGRESS: p. 14.
© LUCASFILM/20TH CENTURY FOX: pp. 97 & 135.
TATE GALLERY, LONDON: pp. 58 & 105.
© WARNER BROS.: pp. 7 & 134.
© WARNER BROS./ORION: p. 112.

# contents

Introduction

# Technicians of Power

In October 2001 enrapt audiences in theaters all over the world watched the movie chronicling the adventures of the young wizard Harry Potter, based on the series of books by J. K. Rowling. A few weeks later even larger throngs gathered to view the first of the *Lord of the Rings* trilogy, in which another wizard, Gandalf the Grey, features largely. For *Harry Potter and the Philosopher's Stone*, the audience was 50 percent children; for *The Lord of the Rings*, 80 percent adult. In both instances the audience was silent and attentive, caught up in these powerful stories that revolved around the world of wizards. The books by J. R. R. Tolkien, on which the *Lord of the Rings* movies are based, are among the most popular books ever written and have been voted the greatest books of the twentieth century in several polls; J. K. Rowling's books are a publishing phenomenon. Both are read with equal enthusiasm by adults and young people alike.

There are many reasons why these books and movies are so popular. They are huge feats of creativity and deeply nourishing stories that satisfy a hunger within us for stories that feed the imagination. But there is another common denominator in both instances: the importance of the part played by wizards. In the Harry Potter stories, we are taken into a world where magic is real and where the young heroes and heroines are taught magic. In Tolkien's books, wizardry plays a hugely important part, and the author developed a specific history relating to his wizards and the magical orders to which they belong. All of these stories, along with countless fantasy books and movies that have built upon works like *The Lord of the Rings*, as well as the medieval cycles of stories concerning King Arthur, continue to occupy a huge space on the shelves of virtually every library and bookstore. Many of them feature wizards

**The archetypal wizard**
The late Richard Harris in the role of the archetypal wizard, Albus Dumbledore, from the movie of *Harry Potter and the Philosopher's Stone*.

**Merlin's cave**
An actor performing the role of
Merlin in the cave below Tintagel
Castle, Cornwall, England. In
Tennyson's epic poem *Idylls of
the King* Merlin finds the infant
Arthur there.

as primary characters, to the point where at least one publisher has stated: "If it doesn't have a wizard in it, I'm not interested!"

What is it that, at the dawn of the twenty-first century, makes us so fascinated by these ancient, archetypal figures? Why do we still find wizards so attractive? Is it because in our hearts we ourselves long to possess magical abilities, to wield a wand of power and speak a single word that can change everything— to be wizards, in fact? Some will think this possible; others will categorically deny it. Whatever the truth, we all, in one way or another, continue to seek out stories that feature wizards, to learn all we can about the way they function and explore the truth about their awesome powers. In the process we can learn a great deal about ourselves and our own, perfectly natural abilities. For the truth is that wizards can offer valuable lessons about the way we live, the way we perceive the universe around us, and the way we relate to others.

**Wands and pointed hats**
The image of a traditional wizard instructing his apprentice in the arts of magic.

This book sets out to answer this need to know and to demonstrate some of the things we can learn from wizards. We look at the long and venerable history of these figures as they appear in different guises around the world. We trace their various incarnations from the fur-clad shamans of the ancient steppe lands to the modern techno-mages of science fiction and movies. We also examine some of the ways that we, as inhabitants of the twenty-first century, can relate to wizards, why we need to relate to them, and how this relationship can change our lives.

The word *wizard* itself comes from the Saxon *wic*, meaning "wise." But other words and titles have become associated with the figure: *magician, sorcerer, magus, mage, alchemist.* All are used to describe the same mysterious, wonder-working, magic-wielding character—though each has its own specific meaning as well. Thus a *magician* is one who deals in magic (and while we are at it, the notion of the conjurer should be banished from our minds at this point; the *wizard* may use slight-of-hand on occasions, but he is no mere trickster). A *sorcerer* is more likely to be a dark magician, one who deals in sorcery, the black arts, who ensorcels or entraps us in webs of lies and deceit. A *magus*, or *mage*, is more often a simple wise man who has perhaps studied the workings of the world and learned that its laws can sometimes be circumvented. An *alchemist* is a protoscientist, an artificer who works on both the physical realm, in attempting to make changes to the world at an elemental level, and the spiritual, in seeking to refine the individual soul.

**Madame Blavatsky**
The nineteenth-century
Russian mystic Madame
Blavatsky frequently
displayed magical skills.

All these may be called *wizards* at certain times, and in this book, more often than not you will find this title used to refer to many different kinds of wonder workers. Wizards can also fulfill the function of the priest, seer, visionary, and artificer. Each of these aspects will be examined in turn throughout the book, offering a nonlinear impression of the wizard based largely on the lives of key figures rather than a chronological account.

While the figure of the wizard is invariably male, those who practice the skillful weaving of magic can be either male or female. The parallel figure of the witch has drawn about her elements of folk magic, herb lore, and midwifery. She is less likely to explore the pursuits of the alchemist and artificer—though in fact several female alchemists are known to have existed, and in our own time such knowledgeable practitioners of magic as the Russian mystic Madame Blavatsky and the British esotericist Dion Fortune have shown that women as well as men can follow the path of the wizard. The common springs of magic remain open to all and have every bit as much to offer women as men.

Magic itself is perceived throughout this book as something as real as any other skill. If nothing else, it can be seen as a microcosmic expression of the macrocosm: humankind's tiny torch of desire uplifted to the fire of the stars. We plug into the universe through the enactment of magic and ritual—beginning with the propitiation of the elements. The wizard builds upon this through the use of a power that can have many different points of origin. He may be more intellectually motivated than the shaman, his focus celestial rather than Earth-based, but his intent is the same. The astrological calculations made by the "star-led wizards" of Milton's "Ode on the Morning of Christ's Nativity" are a far cry from the instinctive actions of the tribal shaman. But each shares a number of basic concepts that would be equally familiar to Merlin or the great Elizabethan magus Dr. John Dee. Only their methods have changed with the movement from tribal to individual consciousness.

The essential task of the wizard is to perfect himself, to follow the dictates of traditions laid down from the earliest times. Through this personal transformation he seeks to perfect the world around him, acting always in tune with age-old precepts, perfectly expressed in the teachings of Hermes Trismegistus (Hermes, as we shall see, created a fountain of wisdom from which all wizards have drunk). The teachings abjured the neophyte to:

> *Leap clear of all that is corporeal, and make yourself*
> *grow to a like expanse with that greatness which is*
> *beyond all measure; rise up above all time, and*
> *become eternal; then you will apprehend God.*

> (*The Corpus Hermeticum*)

Such blazing ideas are the basis for the wizard's work to this day. For wizards are not simply historical figures from ancient times; they may have originated in the past, but they are still very much with us today, in the form of the many people who aspire to the same ideals as those set out in the teachings of Hermes. They may or may not add greatly to the role and character of the wizard, but they share the same sense of purpose, the same desire to bring perfection to themselves and to the world around them.

As you read this book, you may like to think of yourself as apprentice wizards, learning the history and function of your calling just as any neophyte would. To help maintain this idea you will find a number of practices at the end of each chapter, forming a sort of Wizard's Primer, outlining some of the basic practices of the wizard. These exercises may not make actual wizards out of you, but they can give you a sense of what it might feel like to be one and enable you to experience for yourself some of the ancient magic and wisdom possessed by these extraordinary technicians of power.

**The Spell**
A wizard casts a magic circle before performing a ritual summoning in *The Spell* by William Fettes Douglas (1822–1891).

**Gandalf the Grey**
In this painting by John Howe, Gandalf the Grey is portrayed as the archetypal wizard, in the traditional garb of long beard, cloak, and pointed hat, harnessing the power of the elements with his staff.

# 1 | The History of the Wizard from Shaman to Enchanter

# In Search of Wizards

From the farthest West the Wizards come,
And walk among us in the forms of men,
Pretended mortals, thus disguised by some
Few score of years ere they depart again.

DIANA L. PAXSON, *PEOPLE OF POWER*

# The First Ones

Wizards are seekers of wisdom and wielders of a power that comes from being in sync with the universe. Each desires to achieve perfection and, through this, to bring harmony to the world. There are many ways in which they seek to accomplish this goal, differing according to the place or the historical circumstances in which they find themselves. To this end, wizards are also skilled craftspeople, vision seekers, and keepers of knowledge. They can shift shape, create one thing from another, manipulate the elements, and see into the future. They are figures of great strength and mystery.

If most of us were asked to describe a wizard, we would probably come up with "an old man with a long beard dressed in robe and cloak, wearing a pointed hat that has stars on it." We would probably add that he carries a wand or staff and that he possesses a book or books of magic. But most of these details originated over a vast period of time. The first wizards looked nothing like this. Although they were perceived in a very different way, they shared a number of basic characteristics that are still part of the wizard's identity today. They would, for example, have been seen as people who had the ear of God, or of the gods. They could pass at will out of the world of everyday consciousness into another place, generally referred to as the Otherworld. In that place, which was often nonphysical, they acquired information, knowledge, and wisdom that enabled them to tell the future, manipulate the elements, and change their own shape and that of others at will.

The first wizards had all of these skills, but they were called *shamans*, not wizards. They were found all over the world even before recorded history. Their tasks included walking between the worlds, discovering secrets, healing the sick, and foretelling the future. It is to these early and extraordinary beings that we must turn first in our search for the origin and purpose of the wizard.

# Walkers between the Worlds

The shamans were the first guardians and keepers of tradition. They were powerful people who knew how to cooperate with the universe. They could harness the power of the elements to make themselves stronger. Shamans were lore keepers, healers, prophets, diviners, and ceremonialists, as well as ambassadors to and interpreters of the gods. A shaman is born, not made, and only one who was already a shaman could train or guide another. The candidate-shaman would most often receive his or her powers during a spirit journey in which an otherworldly protector or teacher would be encountered. This initiation was undertaken in an isolated place where the candidate would stay to make the first encounter with otherworldly realities. If successful, the initiate would return to the tribe and be inaugurated into the shamanic function by the elders.

Shamans were quite literally walkers-between-worlds whose attunement to both tribal consciousness and that of the gods was so fine that they could slip between the hidden paths of life and death, between this world and the Otherworld. Their personal revelations shaped the tribal consciousness; they formulated and named the gods. It was upon the shamans' revelations and visualizations that the first stirrings of religious practice were built and from which subsequent god-forms and spiritual practices were ultimately derived.

Although there is a great distance in time between the shaman and the magician, there is almost no essential difference in their respective functions. Both stand as mediators of an inner impulse to the outer world. The shaman is a public figure, the center of his tribe's relationship to the gods; the magician is a more secretive figure working often in obscurity but continuing to mediate cosmic forces to his fellow humans. No longer the priest of the tribe, he is constrained into a position of isolation by the dictates of the church; he lives a hidden life that touches that of the person in the street only tangentially. He becomes a shaman-in-civilization, and his magic is the extension of a philosophical and mystical understanding of the universe, rather than the natural, instinctive approach of the shaman.

**Shaman**

A shaman exorcises evil spirits from a sick boy in Alaska at the end of the nineteenth century.

This change took place over a long period, from the Stone Age to the start of the classical era. As humanity progressed and began to formulate its spiritual life around an elected priesthood, the figure of the shaman took a backseat. The roles of doctor, psychiatrist, and seer became split off from the shamans' responsibilities, and they dwindled in most cultures to becoming tribal witch doctors or traditional healers. But the figure of the shaman never totally died out, and our own time has seen a resurgence of interest in their work. The character of the wonder-working magician, however, took on a new guise—that of the wizard. By classical times it had taken a form that is far more recognizable to us today. However, this did not happen overnight. The next stage in the development of the wizard takes us into ancient Jewish and Middle Eastern traditions.

# The Magi and the Magus

Three wizards attended the birth of Christ. The New Testament Greek calls them sages, or wise men, but tradition has called them magi almost from the start. Some commentators have suggested that the word *magic* actually derives from their name. Early Christian iconography depicts them visiting the infant Jesus in a cave, their Phrygian caps identifying them as priests of the Persian god Mithras. Their religion was probably an early form of Zoroastrianism, one of the earliest spiritual impulses to emerge from the Middle East. The Greeks knew and respected them to the point that the word meaning "to be a magus" also meant "to enchant, bewitch, and charm"—all three familiar skills of the wizard. The most famous magi are the three who figure in the familiar Christmas story. They are known as Balthazar, Melchior, and Caspar—the Three Wise Men. Balthazar was of the white race of Shem and brought the gold of incarnation; Melchior was of the black race of Ham and brought the frankincense of crucifixion; Caspar, of the yellow race of Japheth, brought the myrrh of embalming and resurrection. Each stood for a race and an art. Each was an aspect of ancient wisdom coming to pay homage to its newest manifestation. Although they are present at the beginning of Christianity, they are accorded no place in its subsequent development. Yet "they saw the child with Mary, his mother," presumably in much the same way as they would have identified statues of Isis and Horus, Cybele and Attis, and other such prefiguring archetypes. In the presence of the living icon of mother and child, they fell on their knees and worshipped:

**Early signs**
One of the oldest images of a shaman-sorcerer disguised as an animal comes from a prehistoric cave painting in Les Trois Frères, France.

*[They] . . . saw the Virgin holding in her hands Him who with*
*His hands fashioned mankind. Though He had taken*
*the form of a servant, yet they knew Him as their Master.*
*In haste they knelt before Him with their gifts and cried out to the*
*Blessed Virgin: Hail, Mother of the Star that never sets.*

(*The Lenten Triodion,* translated by Mother Mary and Archimandrite Kallistos Ware)

Who were these men who acknowledged Christ as their master before the start of his earthly ministry? One writer describes them as men who were able to understand God, who knew how to minister to the divinity. Others called them "Children of the Chaldeans," referring to an obscure group of protomagicians of whom almost nothing is known beyond the fact that they were the first to develop the arts of astrology and stargazing.

Both descriptions could be applied without alteration to the role of the shaman or the wizard. The magi are still priests, close enough to the gods to recognize a new avatar and to wish to act as intermediaries between divinity and mankind. They are the precursors of the wizards, or perhaps their ancestors, and they bear within them the seeds of that craft. If we look at the histories of certain individuals who are the descendants of both the shaman and the magus, we may begin to see what they have in common—what, in fact, makes them wizards in the first place.

**Magi**
The wise men who visited the infant Jesus were all precursors of wizards from different lands.

# Moses and Magic

**Moses**

Moses listening to the voice of God speaking from a burning bush, and later bringing the Tablets of the Law to his people, in this thirteenth-century manuscript illumination.

oses is not usually considered to be a magician. But, in fact, his life and many of the deeds said to have been performed by him fall into the category of the wizard. He remains a uniquely powerful figure in the religious traditions of both the West and the Middle East, but he is more than simply an inspired leader; in fact, he actually bears many of the hallmarks of the tribal shaman.

The ability of Moses to provide for the Israelites is shown again and again. For example, the gift of the Ten Commandments is obtained after a shamanic-sounding journey to the sacred mountain of Sinai. On other occasions he successfully defeats the sorcerers of the Egyptian Pharaoh, calls down plague and pestilence on the Egyptians, conjures water from a rock, and invokes manna from heaven. His "rod," which may well have been the precursor of the wizard's staff, turns into a snake and back to wood again; he uses it to part the waters of the Red Sea. All of these acts are, of course, attributed to Yahweh, Moses' apocalyptic god. But in each case it is the man, Moses himself, who calls upon the deity to aid him and channels the terrible power that enables him to do these things.

The ability to call upon God, to bring forth such powerful wonders, are all part of the shaman's, and the wizard's, stock-in-trade. Moses' life is filled with portents, signs, and strange events such as often attend the life of a wizard. His preordained birth, his discovery by Pharaoh's daughter, and his later years in the wilderness when he is vouchsafed many visions, which usher in his greatest period of activity in leading the Children of Israel toward the Promised Land, are all signs that he is a wizard with great power. Even his death within sight of the Promised Land and the subsequent mystery that surrounds his burial place are all part of a picture that endures through the history of wizards down to the present day.

# King Solomon's Magic

Moses is not alone among biblical characters in displaying signs of wizardry. King Solomon was also seen as magician—though this aspect of his character has been largely forgotten in the light of his more familiar stock of wisdom. The story of Solomon's election to the kingship of Israel, the famed judgment over the child claimed by two women, the building of the great Temple at Jerusalem, his marriage to Sheba (daughter of the pharaoh)—all these are the stuff of legend and the basis for countless literary retellings, mythical tales, and mysteries.

Here is one such tale taken from early Jewish sources:

## Solomon and the Shamir

Solomon determined to build a great temple to the glory of God. But to do so he had to first find a way to cut and shape the stones, for the law of God said that no stone or tree used to make a sacred place should be hewn with metal, the substance from which weapons were made. Then Solomon remembered the Shamir, a tiny insect, that had the power to cut stone and hew wood and that had carved the writing on the stone tablets brought by Moses from the mountain. However, no one knew where this wondrous creature was to be found.

Solomon thought deeply. Then he touched the mighty ring on his finger and at once a demon appeared before him. "Bring me the Shamir," commanded the king.

The demon cringed. "I cannot, oh, great master. Only our king, Asmodius, knows the whereabouts of the Shamir."

Solomon frowned. "And where is this Asmodius to be found?"

"He lives on a mountaintop far away from here," answered the demon, eager to please. "On the mountain is a wondrous well from which it is his custom to drink daily. Every morning when he leaves he seals it with a rock on which is his mark. Every evening he returns and examines this seal to see that it has not been tampered with. Only then does he drink."

Solomon dismissed the demon with a wave of his hand. Then he summoned the captain of his guard, Benaiah. "I want you to capture the demon Asmodius and bring him to me. Here is a magical ring and a chain of gold inscribed with the holy name of God. Use these to bind him. How you capture him I leave to you."

Benaiah was as wise as he was brave. He set off at once for the mountain where Asmodius lived. When he arrived there he drilled a hole in the rock that covered the well and poured a whole carafe of wine into it. Then he hid close by and watched.

**Solomon**
King Solomon dispenses harsh
wisdom from his throne. Two
women dispute the ownership
of a child; Solomon threatens to
cut the infant in two and the real
mother cries out. William Blake's
*The Judgement of Solomon* (1800).

As the sun set, the demon arrived. Terrible and black he was, with horns that sprouted from every joint in his body. He examined the seal on the well and, finding it unbroken and failing to notice the little hole, he raised the stone and drank deeply. Being unused to wine, he quickly fell into a deep sleep. At once Benaiah emerged from hiding and bound the demon with the golden chain, sealing it with Solomon's ring of power.

When the demon woke, he found that he could not move.

"Who has done this?" he thundered.

"I have," said Benaiah. "My master, King Solomon, demands to see you."

Asmodius could not refuse, and by his power they went swiftly to Solomon's palace. There the demon trembled before the master of all spirits.

"I seek the Shamir," said Solomon.

"That you will never do," answered Asmodius. "The Shamir is under the protection of the King of the Sea, and he has placed it in the care of the woodcock, whose nest is on top of a mountain."

Then Solomon again summoned Benaiah. "I have a new task for you. The Shamir is to be found on a far distant mountain, in the nest of the woodcock. I bid you journey there and bring it back with you." Then the king gave him a box lined with lead and a thick pane of glass and instructed him how they were to be used.

**Solomon meets Belial**

The demon Belial, a Prince of Hell, pays reluctant homage to King Solomon in this twelfth-century English illustration.

Benaiah set off once more and journeyed until he came to the mountain described by Asmodius. This he climbed until he came to the place where the woodcock had its nest. There, just as Solomon's wisdom had perceived, he found some of the bird's nestlings left alone.

As his master had told him to do, Benaiah placed the pane of glass over the nest and then hid himself nearby. Soon the bird returned and found its chicks imprisoned beneath the glass. Screaming harshly, the woodcock hammered at the glass with its beak, but in vain.

When it saw that this was of no use, the bird took the tiny Shamir from under its wing and laid it upon the glass. As soon as the insect touched it, the glass cracked into pieces. At that moment Benaiah leaped out of his hiding place, seized the insect, and thrust it into the lead-lined box. Then he set off for home.

With the help of the wonderful insect, King Solomon was able to cut the stones he needed to build the great Temple to the glory of God. And men say that he was helped in this by Asmodius and his kin. But of the Shamir nothing more is known.

✦  ✦  ✦  ✦  ✦

Beneath stories of this kind, which describe an all-wise king, prophet, and lawgiver, lies a substratum of material describing a tribal shaman or wizard of enormous power. From the legends that came to surround him, we hear that during his childhood Solomon was subject to attack by the evil spirit Beelzebub; that God gave him a magical ring with four stones that gave him control over the elements, over all birds and beasts, over all men, and over spirits (terrestrial, celestial, and infernal)—making him indeed the most powerful wizard of that or any time.

We also hear that in his later years Solomon was prey to great lust and that this led him to renounce Yahweh and turn to other, darker gods. He is said to have written a number of books of magic that, although he later tried to destroy them, survived to become the source of much latter-day magic.

Though Solomon's ring is long since lost to the world, the three surviving books attributed to him, which are part of the tradition on which modern-day ritual magic is based, may be read by anyone in modern translations. Regardless of their authenticity, they paint a picture of Solomon as wielding extraordinary power that has seldom if ever been equaled. From him comes the wizard's book of spells, magic ring, and ability to commune with the spirits. In addition, Solomon's connection with the Freemasons and the many mysteries surrounding the building of the Temple at Jerusalem have added an even deeper color to the character of this remarkable figure.

# Thrice Greatest Hermes

The next major players in the history of the wizard come from the classical worlds of Greece and Rome. These wizards display a more intellectual approach to the understanding of the universe and its magical manipulation. They are more often perceived as philosophers rather than mages, equally at home seeking out the tides and patterns of life as they are evoking spirits and controlling the power of wind and wave.

The great foundation stone upon which not only their work but that of most subsequent followers of the wizard's path is based is the figure of Hermes Trismegistus ("Thrice Greatest"). This composite being inherited the teachings and characteristics of the Egyptian Thoth and the Greek Hermes—both gods representing universal wisdom and magic. Hermes is thrice great because he is philosopher, king, and priest, roles that can still be perceived within the archetype of the wizard. Legend describes Hermes as a king who lived 3,226 years and carried with him an emerald on which he had inscribed a synthesis of all wisdom. This so-called Emerald Tablet is believed to be hidden in Hermes' long-lost tomb, but at some point it was transcribed— though no two translations (most originating in the late classical period) are exactly the same. Nonetheless, the ideas set out in this remarkable text influenced the thinking and beliefs of wizards up to the present time, and continue to do so.

**Hermes**

Hermes Trismegistus teaches the magical wisdom of the Emerald Tablet to his disciples in this fifteenth-century image from Sienna, Italy.

The nine marvelous precepts that make up the Emerald Tablet illustrate its all-inclusive language, which has been read as equally applicable to both pagan and Christian students of magic:

I  In truth certainly and without doubt, whatever is below is like that which is above, and whatever is above is like that which is below, to accomplish the miracles of one thing.

2  Just as all things proceed from one alone by meditation on one alone, so also they are born from this one thing by adaptation.

3  Its father is the sun and its mother is the moon. The wind has borne it in its body. Its nurse is the earth.

4  It is the father of every miraculous work in the whole world.

5  Its power is perfect if it is converted into earth.

6  Separate the earth from the fire and the subtle from the gross softly and with great prudence.

7  It rises from earth to heaven and comes down again from heaven to earth and thus acquires the power of the realities below. In this way you will acquire the glory of the whole world, and all darkness will leave you.

8  This is the power of all powers, for it conquers everything subtle and penetrates everything solid.

9  Thus the little world is created according to the prototype of the great world.

From this profound text springs 90 percent of the magical work and practice of the wizard from this time forward. Throughout the ages he has sought to reshape the "little world" in which we all live according to the plan of the "great world," by whatever name or in whatever form we choose to perceive it. This was the work of the magician from the beginning, and it continues to be so in our own time.

# The Philosopher Mage

Perhaps the greatest of the classical magicians to be influenced by the ideas of Hermes Trismegistus is Pythagoras, a figure more associated with philosophy than magic. Yet his life and the stories that grew up around him reflect those of wizards in a number of ways. In common with a number of classical magicians, he is said to have been a demigod, possibly begotten by Apollo himself. The reality of this refers to a spiritual lineage as much as to a literal descent. Pythagoras was said to have inherited the physical beauty of the god, along with a precocity that distinguishes extraordinary, god-born mortals. While Pythagoras was still a child, his teacher, Tales, declared he could teach him nothing and sent him to Egypt to study the mysteries. Recognized as a semi-immortal by the Egyptian priesthood, he received their teachings before being captured and carried into captivity in Babylon. There he became a follower of Zoroaster, thus combining within himself a confluence of Western and Eastern doctrine and magic.

It was to be forty years—always a significant number in the process of initiation—before Pythagoras returned to Greece. On the way he stopped at the island of Crete and visited the cave on Mount Ida, which was sacred to his father, Apollo, and to Zeus. He remained in the cave for twenty-seven days, during which he claimed to have visited the Otherworld. On returning he began teaching the doctrine of the transmigration of souls, for which he is still remembered today. He also founded a secret society of believers who were put through a series of initiatory tests to prove themselves worthy.

Soon after this, Pythagoras fell into the hands of a tyrant named Phalaris, who put him on trial for the practice of wizardry. Pythagoras's disciple Abaris defended him in court and was himself imprisoned. But on the day when they were both condemned to die, Phalaris was killed and the two philosopher-magicians were released. Conflicting accounts exist of the eventual death of Pythagoras. Some say that he was burned to death along with a number of his followers in a fire started by a disaffected disciple who had been forbidden entrance to the master's inner circle. Others report his flight to Metapontum, where he apparently vanished into a narrow valley that was said to lead directly to the Otherworld.

Pythagoras's primary magical power was his ability to control the natural world. He was able to tame a wild bear by whispering in its ear, catch and disarmed serpents, and was hailed as a wonder-worker by Nessus, god of the river Euenos. A life written by the third-century philosopher Iamblicus reports that he made

*infallible predictions of earthquakes, rapid expulsions of pestilence, instantaneous cessation of the effusion of hail, and a tranquilization of the rivers and seas, in order that his disciples might pass over them.*

**Pythagoras**

The Greek philosopher-magician Pythagoras emerges from a cave on Mount Ida after visiting the Otherworld in this painting by Salvator Rosa (1622).

# VIRGIL THE WIZARD

O f all the great classical wizards the most unusual, as well as the most famous, is surely the Roman poet Virgil. In his lifetime he had no actual association with magic. However, in the Middle Ages he became transformed through a series of misunderstandings of his work into a figure possessed of magical powers and a number of fantastic adventures. Reports of various miracles that took place in and around Virgil's tomb within a hundred years of his death promoted him from poet to mystic to virtual god, and soon stories began to circulate that substantiated these claims.

**Virgil**
After his death, the Roman poet Virgil was widely believed to have been a magician. Here he leads another poet, Dante Aligheri, through the Underworld in a scene from Dante's great poem *The Inferno*.

First, Virgil was given a miraculous birth story, with the ground beneath the city of Rome shaking on the day of his nascence. His extreme precocity made it clear that he was destined to become a major figure in Roman history. The story went that he accidentally encountered a powerful spirit trapped in a hole in the ground. The spirit offered him a copy of Solomon's book of magic in return for his release. Virgil accepted the book but used its contents to trick the evil spirit into reentering its hole. Now possessed of great magical powers, Virgil entered into a magical battle against the Roman emperor's sorcerer. When he was victorious, Virgil regained the lands that the senate had stolen from him.

Virgil was said to have used his magic powers to conduct a love affair with the daughter of the sultan of Babylon, visiting her by creating a bridge of air from his home in Naples to Persia. Later he built her a magic castle in which to live. But he gave her hand in marriage to one of his knights because he preferred to maintain his own freedom.

The story of this semimythical Virgil's death is as bizarre as the stories of his birth and life.

**Virgil's tomb**
The tomb of Virgil in Naples, Italy, was the scene of miracles and other strange occurrences within a hundred years of the poet's death.

## THE DEATH OF VIRGIL

As he grew old Virgil decided to cheat death by renewing his youth. But the way this was to be achieved was terrible indeed. Calling to him his most trusted servant, the magician gave him these instructions: "First you must cut up my body into seven parts. Place the pieces in beds of salt for seven days. Then you must place all the pieces into a cauldron, which I shall have prepared. From this I shall come forth renewed."

In great fear and trembling the servant did as he was bid, cutting the body of his master into pieces and laying each one carefully in a bed of salt. Then he sat by to wait the passing of seven days, all the time tending the great cauldron in which his master had placed certain herbs and other ingredients too terrible to name.

Then on the fifth day there came a great hammering on the doors of Virgil's house. It was the emperor himself, who, having missed his prophet, had come to find him. When he saw the poet's severed head, he feared the worst. The servant pleaded in terror, but the emperor had him killed at once. As the servant died, the emperor saw what seemed to be a naked child running around the cauldron crying: "Cursed be the day you came!" before it disappeared entirely. It was the wizard's reborn soul, which, having no body to return to, was lost forever.

✦ ✦ ✦ ✦ ✦

Later reports mention that, within a few years of his death, Virgil's writings were being used to make divinations. His texts would be opened at random and a finger would be placed on a line, which was then used to answer a prefigured question. It was widely believed that the poet had prophesied the coming of Christ in his *Fourth Eclogue*, which prompted Dante to make Virgil his guide through the underworld in *The Divine Comedy*. This most unlikely wizard is really the product of imagination and invention, but nonetheless Virgil became a central figure who bridged the gap between the ancient world and the Middle Ages.

# Wizards of
# the Middle Ages

Medieval wizards and magicians seem positively backward compared with their classical forebears, few emulating the kind of feats attributed to Apollonius or Solomon. This was in part due to the influence of medieval scholasticism, the intellectual arm of the church in Europe. It governed the physical forms of knowledge—books, manuscripts, and documents— kept under its scrutiny, making them conform to Christian views. Here the wizard had no place, although it is ironic that the conventional stereotype of the magus as a celestially cloaked individual conjuring demons into a triangle from a safe distance really originates from this time. In reality, these demons were *daemons* (spiritual helpers) esoterically akin to angels, who communicated the wisdom of higher worlds. Psychologically, we might observe that magicians who resorted to such methods of conjuration were actually recognizing and integrating those aspects of themselves that communed with an Otherworld reality. To treat the helpful daemon as a demon was to struggle with those inner aspects of the self that were as yet unbalanced or unintegrated. Negative individual aspects were demonic, whereas good aspects were polarized as angelic; the unintegrated aspects remained bound in the triangle of conjuration forever.

But the medieval era is characterized by a sense of curiosity, and it was this that enabled the wizard to reestablish a place in the imagination of the world. Medieval scholars wanted to know how the world worked, even if the church officially forbade them to ask. Alchemy flourished under these difficult conditions, and scientific investigation was a force to be reckoned with, despite being curtailed by Rome. One of the most important medieval wizards, Roger Bacon (c. 1214–1292) was actually a Franciscan monk. Yet he managed, in an extraordinary way, to become an almost archetypal wizard figure for his time. Really a protoscientist, he did not exclude magic from his studies but allowed it to contain at least "some truth."

In his own cautious way, Bacon was more of a wizard than many of his more notorious fellows. He shares with Virgil the curious honor of being called a worker of marvels after his death. His magic mirror enabled him to see what was happening anywhere in the world. He also consulted a "brazen head," which would answer any question put to it. Given Bacon's farsighted genius, this may be more accurately perceived to be the world's first computer rather than a magical implement. But this is not to say that we should dismiss its creator from our list of wizards. There has always been a practical, inquisitive side to magic, as we shall see, and Bacon's lively mind represents this as well as any who came before or after him.

ꝟ ſeneſceute ſeueſauit hoies noū ꝓpter ununi
ſeueetutem ſ̃ multiplici͌ ꝟmenau̅ uiſiaeuci
ꝙ̄m aerem qu̅ nos aunnō̃at ⁊ ueſigenaa regis ⁊
noꝛanaa i͟ꝰ res. ꝓetatunꝙ que regis ꝛeſtrn ſuplent

Bacon certainly studied the magical books, called *grimoires*, that circulated in enlightened circles, and he wrote a treatise called *The Mirror of Alchemy*, which contains much that would not be out of place in any wizard's handbook. He seems to have taken to heart words attributed to St. Jerome by another medieval writer, Gerald of Wales, that refer to a kind of natural magic present in the world: "You will find many things quite incredible and beyond the bounds of probability which are true for all that. Nature never exceeds the limits set by God, who created it."

**Roger Bacon**
The thirteenth-century monk and scientist Roger Bacon acquired a reputation as a wizard during his lifetime. He wrote one of the earliest treatises on magic.

**Merlin the Wise**

Merlin sleeps under the spell
of the sorceress Vivien in this
nineteenth-century illustration
by E. F. Brickdate of Tennyson's
*Idylls of the King*.

# Merlin the Wise

Perhaps the most famous magician of all time is as much a product of the Middle Ages as any of the figures we have been examining. He is, of course, Merlin, who is best known as King Arthur's enchanter. This mysterious figure is said to have "created" the Round Table and acted as adviser to the young king until he was seduced and trapped under a hawthorn tree by the sorceress Nimue. In the light of his extraordinary qualities and legendary status, it is perhaps not surprising that he embodies many of the role changes through which the character of the wizard has passed.

The earliest references to Merlin describe him as a prophet—living in the wilds of the Caledonian forest, talking to animals, and foretelling events to come. As such he is still something of a shamanic figure, but from then on he develops quite quickly into the mage and wonder-worker of the Arthurian cycle. Geoffrey of Monmouth, a twelfth-century cleric, compiled a book of Merlin's prophecies that became something of a best-seller. Geoffrey responded to this by writing *The History of the Kings of Britain*, in which Merlin was seen as already in place as a wonder-working child and subsequently as adviser to Arthur. This was followed a few years later by *The Life of Merlin*, which combined the older figure with that of the medieval wizard. His knowledge of the elemental magic of wood, water, and sky probably derives from distant recollections of the Celtic druids, to whom similar skills were attributed from the time of Julius Caesar and in the literature of medieval Ireland.

A typical story of Merlin describes his love of tricks and disguises—methods often used by the great wizards to teach valuable lessons.

# MERLIN APPEARS TO KING ARTHUR

O ne day, not long after he became king, Arthur grew tired of the life at court and decided to escape for a day into the great wood that lay beneath the walls of his city. Taking his finest horse, he slipped out of a side gate and rode all day until the sun began to set. Then he stopped to rest beside a well of sweet water and saw a most wonderful thing.

First he heard a noise like the baying of hounds; then there came in view the strangest creature Arthur had ever seen. It had the head of a serpent, the body of a leopard, the tail of a snake, and the feet of a hart, and as it moved, the sound of baying hounds came from inside it.

The strange beast came right up to the well and bent its head to drink. Only then did the noise cease; but as soon as it had finished drinking the barking began again. With a shake of its head the beast continued on its way, passing from sight amid the trees.

Filled with wonder, the young king sat by the well until he saw a young boy coming along the way. "I expect you are wondering about that beast you saw," said the child. "In truth I am," replied Arthur, "but I do not believe for a moment that you can know anything about it. You are far too young."

The child shrugged his shoulders and went on his way.

Shortly after, an old man with a long white beard came into view.

"Do you know anything about that strange beast that passed this way?" asked Arthur.

"That I do," answered the old man. "But you didn't want to hear it when I looked like a child!" So saying, he cast off the illusion with which he had cloaked himself, and there stood Merlin, the king's own enchanter.

Arthur had the grace to feel ashamed, but the wizard forgave him, deeming he had learned a lesson. As for the wondrous beast, Merlin told him that it was called the Questing Beast, and that only those of pure heart and great determination could follow it, and that one day a good man named Pelinore would capture it. "But that is a long time away," said Merlin. "And now you have a kingdom to rule, my liege."

**The Questing Beast**
The young King Arthur sleeps beneath a tree while the strange Questing Beast drinks from a stream. Merlin will later interpret the meaning of this as the beginning of a great quest.

Cloaked in mystery, appearing and disappearing in various shapes at will, moving in and out of the stories of Arthur and his fellowship in a completely unpredictable manner, Merlin is described as possessing ever more awesome powers. He can call forth whole pageants of imaginary beings from the air and dismiss them with consummate ease. Ultimately he became the preeminent power in the land during Arthur's reign, credited with orchestrating the mysteries the Grail and of the various quests undertaken by the Round Table knights.

Throughout the Renaissance, Merlin remained an important figure whose *Prophecies*, updated in each generation by willing neophytes, were standard fare in the houses of the well-to-do. In our own time his character influenced George Lucas in the creation of his own "wizard" figure, *Star Wars'* Obi-Wan-Kenobi, while T. H. White's classic story *The Once and Future King*, the basis for the musical *Camelot*, has influenced a whole generation of fantasy authors whose wizardly creations continue to appear on the shelves of libraries and bookstores around the world.

**Merlin and King Arthur**

Merlin became King Arthur's most trusted adviser. Here he introduces the knight Sir Galahad to the Round Table fellowship.

# †HE DIVIⱧE DOCTOR

If Merlin is the archetypal medieval wizard, Dr. John Dee must be considered his equal in importance if not in power during the Elizabethan Renaissance. Dee was probably the single most influential aspect of the magician ever to have lived and a worthy successor to the Arthurian mage.

Born in 1527, Dee rose from comparative obscurity to a position of power as adviser and court astrologer to Elizabeth I. He is considered to have been the foremost mathematician of his day. He traveled widely and left an abundance of writings. His diaries and notebooks testify to his largesse of spirit, depth of occult understanding, and qualities of perception. Born while Henry VIII was still on the throne, he lived on into the age of James I, surviving five reigns and five changes of religious allegiance in that troubled age. He died finally in 1608, all but forgotten by the world that he had subtly influenced for so long. During his long life he synthesized much that has come to be accepted as an integral part of the magical tradition and hence of the wizard's stock of lore: neo-Platonism and Pythagorianism, kabbala, alchemical, and hermetic traditions were molded into an intricate system of correspondences along with lengthy lists of angelic beings with whom Dee claimed to have spoken. His influence on the statesman-poet Sir Philip Sidney and his circle, a group Shakespeare called the School of Night, was considerable, and through him may well have come the cult of the Virgin Queen that became attached to Elizabeth.

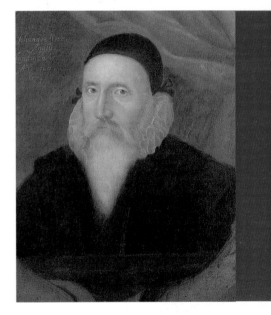

**Dr. John Dee**

Dr. Dee, an astrologer who advised Queen Elizabeth I of England throughout her reign, played a major role in the history of the wizard.

Dee can be seen as a prime example of the wizard in the political arena because he transmitted inner impulses to the outer world, which is always a foremost task of the magician. Moving in a twilight realm of mystery and wonder, Dee no longer worked solely with elementals or demons. Instead he held converse with spiritual entities of a higher order that he called angels. Within the confines of his circle, Dee would still call up spirits from the vasty deep, but they were of another order now, and the reasons for calling them had changed as well. Dee was no longer interested in occult lore for its own sake, but had recognized that it offered a means to further his own career. For a few years his star was in the ascendant, and he became the most sought-after astrologer and seer of his age. But in the end scandal and rumor ruined him, and he ended his life in poverty, begging for crumbs from the royal table that had once so liberally sustained him.

# Modern-Day Wizards

Though many famous wizards followed Dee, notably Count Cagliostro in the eighteenth century, none added significantly to the central image. Figures in the nineteenth and twentieth centuries included Aleister Crowley (1875–1947), who was dubbed (probably by himself!) "the wickedest man alive," as well as Gregory Rasputin, the Russian monk whose influence over the czar and czarina made him famous.

Crowley did much to publicize—often unflatteringly—the character of the modern-day wizard by living life to the full and creating a cloud of sensationalism around his sexual exploits. Others, such as Madame Blavatsky, who founded the Theosophical Society in 1875, probably belong more to the world of mystics than magicians. However, Blavatsky was said to have performed more than one magical act, such as the time she visited someone in the hospital and apparently conjured a bunch of fresh roses (out of season) into the sickroom.

The Hermetic Order of the Golden Dawn, founded in 1888 by MacGregor Mathers, A. E. Waite, and Aleister Crowley, among others, became a focus for a number of adepts and wizards living in Britain. At one time it numbered the poet W. B. Yeats among its ranks. Another member, Israel Regardie (1907–1985), was for a while Crowley's secretary and wrote a number of influential books on the practice of ritual magic. Another sometime member was Dion Fortune (1890–1946), who founded a magical school, the Society of the Inner Light, in 1923.

Even more recently, a number of latter-day wizards have embraced the dream and intention of the historical wizard, teaching these skills to eager apprentices around the world and establishing their own magical groups. Gareth Knight, who was a member of Dion Fortune's Society of the Inner Light, went on to found his own order and was one of the first practicing magicians to bring the occult work of the magician into the public domain through the holding of a number of workshops in which rituals were enacted. W. E. Butler (1898–1978) took up the kabbalistic magic of the society and promoted it widely throughout Europe and North America. Butler studied not only with Dion Fortune but also with Hindu spiritual teachers and with the well-known mystic Annie Besant. He was cofounder of another modern magical order, the Servants of the Light Association. After his death the leadership of this group passed to Dolores Ashcroft-Nowicki, herself a highly trained magical practitioner, who has continued to promote the work of the modern wizard in the outer world as well as the inner, through the medium of a popular correspondence course and workshops, which she presents all over the world.

**Aleister Crowley**
Aleister Crowley (1875–1947) was the most famous wizard of his day. He called himself "The Great Beast" and made extravagant claims of his occult powers.

All this has served to give the character and personality of the wizard an active place in our own time. There has probably never been a period in history when so many famous wizards have held us in thrall with their adventures and taught us with their wisdom—though these are more likely to reach us (at least initially) in the pages of books or on the celluloid screen. The reason for this continuing fascination is almost as subtle as the wizards themselves. It derives— at least in part—from an increasing desire to understand our place in the universe and to find out what makes the universe tick. In the following chapters we will look at some of the ways that wizards have enchanted us through the ages—as visionaries, wisdom-keepers, artisans, protoscientists, and elemental masters— and at the way in which their role has reflected a growing awareness of the world in which we live.

One thing is certain: Wizards are here to stay, and their presence—whether in the worlds of the occult, literature, cinema, or scientific discovery—continues to enrich our lives at virtually every level.

# İMAGİNE YOURSELF A WİZARD

I t is far from easy to become a practicing wizard today, despite the fact that there are many people and groups who offer training in the occult arts. To become a wizard requires years of intense and often difficult work, much of it exhausting and—it must be said— far from exciting. Until you have sat at your desk learning the multitude of angelic names associated with magical conjuration or the correspondences of the spheres and pathways on the kabbalistic tree of life as a means to enhance your magical abilities, you cannot imagine how monotonous this kind of work can be. It can be rewarding, to be sure, but it is still monotonous. In a book of this kind you will not find instructions on how to become a wizard, but you can catch a glimpse of what that training would be like. In the visualization that follows, you will find yourself following a scenario that takes you through some of the stages in a wizard's training and offers personal insights into your own life.

The way to get the most from any visualization is to be as present to the experience as possible. Be inside it rather than watching it on a TV screen in your head. Sit where you can be comfortable and undisturbed but not so comfortable that you fall asleep. Read the text of the visualization through once or twice until you are familiar with it. Then close your eyes, take a few deep breaths, and replay the images described in the text with yourself at the center. Keep a notebook and pen close at hand to write down any insights that come to you. Alternatively, you might like to read the text into a tape recorder and play it back to yourself.

See before you a large, wooden, nail-studded door. On it is a handle depicting a strange face—half human, half lion—with a ring gripped in its mouth. Reach up and turn the handle and push the door. It opens silently and you enter a small chamber lined with panels of dark wood. There is a fireplace in which burns a cheerful fire, and an ancient, ornate mirror hangs above it. There is a chair and a table on which lie ancient books piled up haphazardly along with a number of strangely shaped beakers and alembics such as you might see in a laboratory. A large oak chest stands in one corner, and you go across to this now and open it. Within is a neat pile of clothes. You unfold the garments and find they are dark blue robes, edged at neck and hem with white fur. You put them on over your own clothing. At the bottom of the chest is a flat-topped hat made of velvet. You put this on and then look at yourself in the mirror above the fireplace. There you see your own face, but it is somehow changed—not only because of the unfamiliar clothes but in a deeper way. It is as if by donning the robes and hat of the wizard you have taken upon you a role and character different from your usual self.

Turning away from the mirror, you sit at the table and open one of the books. Its contents are surprising. You find that you can read them even though they are written in an old-fashioned hand in what you take to be Latin. The most surprising thing about the words is that they contain your own name. As you read, you find that they describe your own life—but with subtle differences. This life is similar to the one you remember in this world, except that here you have undertaken the training of a wizard. The book is an account of your experiences. It mentions learning how to read the signs of the future, how to protect yourself against dark magic, how to make a talisman, and how to work with the elements. Read it carefully and look out for particular incidents that strike a chord within you. . . .

The final entry in the book informs you that you have a task to perform, a spell to cast, or a potion to make. This is for something that is appropriate to your own life at this moment, something you would like to change or improve—always remembering to consider anyone else that the change might affect.

You close the book and look around the chamber. In another corner, half hidden in the dim light, you see a cupboard. Crossing the room, you open it. Within are ingredients, strange and wonderful things in bottles and containers. Using your intuitive skills and without thought, take out a number of these. Take them to the table and begin to mix them in one of the glass alembics. As you do this, still relying on intuitive thought, listen for a phrase or verse that will come to you. . . .

Once the potion or spell is complete, sit down again at the table and open the book. Then write down everything you remember of the preparation. Concentrate on the piece of work you intend to do. . . .

When you open your eyes, you see that the room has changed. It seems bigger now, and there is another door opening on the far side from the one by which you entered. You cross to this and open it. Beyond is a small garden with high walls around it and many beds of aromatic herbs. Go outside and, again using your intuition, choose three herbs and bring them back into the room. Over the fire now hangs an ancient cauldron full of bubbling water. Throw the herbs into this and breathe in their aroma, which slowly begins to fill the room. You then begin to feel sleep coming over you. You close your eyes and begin to dream. . . . Whatever you see in this dream contains a message for you. . . .

In no time at all, it seems, you are awake again and find yourself back where you began the visualization. Write down anything you can remember, either from the book of your training or the dream that followed. See if you can bring to mind any part of the spell or potion you prepared. Remember how it felt to be a wizard working in the world of magic. In the exercises that you find throughout this book, you have a chance to experience some of the same things of which you read in the ancient book, but this time they will take place in your everyday life.

## Stonehenge

According to one account, Merlin was responsible for setting up the great circle of stones known today as Stonehenge. Though historically untrue, this shows the power ascribed to the wizard.

2 | The Wizard as Prophet and Visionary

# Those Who See in the Dark

*This prophecy shall Merlin make; for I live before his time.*

SHAKESPEARE, *KING LEAR: ACT 3, SCENE 2*

## Druids and Seers

For as long as we can remember we have, as a species, sought to know what the future holds in store for us, what lies around the next corner. Unable to do this for ourselves, we have sought out the professional seers whose task it is to look into the darkness of the future and bring light to bear upon it. The history of the wizard is inextricably bound up with traditions of seership and vision. Those who could divine or tell the future were accorded a unique status from earliest times. The shamans, as we saw earlier, literally kept the life of the tribe in their hands in this way, and those who inherited this role wielded great power. Since then, the ability of wizards to foretell future events has remained one of their most important abilities, as well as a central aspect of their aim to bring perfection to themselves and the world.

The prophetic tradition among the Celts, for example, was very highly developed, the primary fuel for this being the search for inspiration. Stories about finding *imbas* (Irish) or *awen* (Welsh)—both words for "inspiration"—are at the heart of the seer's work, and also the wizard's. For the Celtic seers, imbas resided in the salmon of knowledge that swam in a well that rose in the Otherworld; awen was sought in the inspirational draught of cauldrons owned by gods or goddesses—their gift to transform those who drank their sometimes perilous draught. Inspiration is regarded as a spirit to be sought by the practitioner, courted under a variety of metaphors, such as a fish, rushing water, hazelnuts, a spiral tower, a net of stars, a fairy woman. The results of the union between inspiration and the practitioner are described in metaphors of abundance, overwhelming waters, vigorous energy, and vortices of light.

The druids are people who in some senses bridge the gap between the ancient shamans and the later medieval image of the wizard. Contention still rages over their origins, but they exist to this day in the form of various neo-Druidic revivalist orders. Whatever their place of origin or whenever they appeared, they are known to have been remarkable visionaries. They also possessed powers that are now part and parcel of the wizard's stock-in-trade.

A separate order within the Druidic hierarchy, the Ovates (from the Latin *vates*) or seers had the task of recording the inner history of the people, of seeking the answers to questions posed both by individuals and the community. How they did this is a closely guarded secret, and since they chose to commit their wisdom to memory rather than to writing, descriptions of their abilities are few and far between. However, some have survived, albeit from a later time. An account by a ninth-century cleric named Cormac reads:

> *The [seer] discovers . . . whatever he likes or desires to reveal. This is the way in which it is done: the [seer] chews a bit of the flesh of a red pig, or of a dog, and he conveys it afterwards to the flag (stone) behind the door and pronounces an incantation on it, and offers it to idol gods, and then invokes his idols; and if he obtains not his desire on the day following, he pronounces incantations over both his palms, and invokes again unto him his idol gods, in order that his sleep may not be interrupted; and he lays his two palms on his two cheeks, and falls asleep; and he is watched, in order that no one may interrupt or disturb him, until everything about which he is engaged in is revealed to him.*

Cormac is describing a practice that had been forbidden in his day and shows hesitation about some parts of the procedure, yet he clearly tells us about the sharing of meat with the spirits and a subsequent incubation of the question in a monitored sleep or entranced state. The laying of the palms over the cheeks ensures that the fingers are shielding the eyes from light—a primary requisite for both sleep and the seeking of the vision.

A twelfth-century chronicler, Gerald of Wales, gives biblical examples of prophecy, then concludes, "You will object that the prophets were not possessed when they prophesied, whereas we read that when Merlin Silvester [i.e., Merlin the Wild] made his prophecies he was in a frenzy, and in the same way the other soothsayers about whom I have written . . . seem to be possessed." This notion of the possession and seeming madness of the prophet is a common one. It is part of the seer's ability to leave behind ordinary consciousness while keeping one foot on the earth. Gerald's words lead us to a consideration of some of the more prophetic figures whose skill as seers is central to their importance in the lineage of the wizard.

# Apollonius and the Emperor

O ne of the greatest and most visionary wizards of any era was Apollonius of Tyana, who flourished in the first century C.E. Like his master, the philosopher-mage Pythagoras, he was considered by some to have been a god. He is said to have been begotten by Proteus, god of the winds and patron of shape-shifters, which was an appropriate choice

**Apollonius**
Apollonius of Tyana, here depicted with the symbols of his prophetic and occult power, was a guardian of ancient wisdom.

for the father of a wizard. Apollonius possessed miraculous powers that enabled him, among other things, to prophesy accurately the deaths of several Roman emperors. On a number of occasions he narrowly escaped death at the hands of the angry priesthoods of various cults with whom he came into conflict. He is also said to have visited Hades, to inquire of the god of the Underworld what was the most pure philosophy then available to humankind. He traveled extensively, performing feats that defied rational explanation, and vanished mysteriously after a long life. Many of his contemporaries compared him with Christ and found him superior, while others regarded him as a figure of evil. In his writings he speaks of methods of "tying" and "untying" the elements through the pronouncement of the secret names of God—a method of magical practice that is fascinatingly similar to that of the Jewish kabbalistic magicians of a later age.

Apollonius stands out as a representative of the wizard as seer. Despite warnings, he faced the mad Emperor Nero (whose overthrow he had prophesied) and survived. He then made a number of accurate prophecies regarding the deaths of no less than five emperors. When this came to the ears of the next reigning ruler of Rome, Domitian (C.E. 81–96), he promptly had Apollonius imprisoned on the grounds that he had predicted that the emperor would be struck down by avenging gods. When he stood at last before Domitian, Apollonius was calm and self-possessed:

*"Lord," he said, "what support shall I ask for in my defense? I shall invoke the memory of your father, Vespasian, who visited me in Egypt before he became emperor. It was I who prophesied to him his future greatness. You are therefore under a natural obligation to me, following him on the throne. I used no enchantments to excite him to attempt the conquest of the empire; I never flattered myself in his presence with statements that*

> *I could alter the course of the sun at my pleasure nor change the progress*
> *of human events. . . . Give ear no longer to vile spies who accuse me of*
> *conspiring against you. . . . Condemn me now if it is your caprice, but*
> *know that my destiny is not made to perish at your hands."*
>
> Christian, *The History and Practice of Magic*

Domitian, to whom no one had ever dared speak in this way, turned pale and remained frozen in his seat. The mage of Tyana slowly left the Pretorium and went from the city of Rome unpunished.

Some time after this, as Apollonius was teaching at Ephesus, he suddenly fell silent and leaned to one side, like a man listening. Then he walked three or four steps and made a gesture of command, saying: "Strike! Strike! The gods command it!" The audience thought he had been attacked by some kind of feverish delirium, but rising to his full height, he told them, in a thunderous voice: "Ephesians, it is done. At the moment in which I now speak to you the tyrant has fallen and I see Rome on its feet, acclaiming its liberty!" A few days later the news of the murder of Domitian reached Ephesus, and the time indicated by Apollonius was exactly that at which the emperor had fallen with seven knife wounds.

Such abilities set Apollonius apart from other wizards of the classical era. He never fully explained his prophetic gifts, but he did declare that he once stood in the presence of a divine representative of the ancient Egyptian mysteries, a goddess who gave him powers that most wizards would have been happy to claim. The words quoted by him are both extraordinary and moving:

> *I am the daughter of the past and the mother of the future; I am the queen*
> *of the spirits and God's reflection on earth and in all the worlds. . . . If you*
> *have the courage to follow me to the heights where Truth abides, I shall*
> *make a new man of you; I shall give you new eyes which shall be opened*
> *upon the infinite world of immortal essences. You shall measure all time*
> *with a single glance; you shall embrace all beings as one, in a single*
> *thought; the divine powers shall reveal their secrets to you and the forces*
> *of nature shall obey you.*

The last words perfectly state the nature of the prophetic and visionary abilities expressed by so many of the wizards discussed here. They would have fittingly described the abilities of Merlin, who was as great a prophet as he was a worker of magic.

# Merlin the Prophet

The story of Merlin's visionary gifts is explored in the twelfth-century book by Geoffrey of Monmouth, *The History of the Kings of Britain*. Here the story of Merlin's first appearance as a child of no more than nine years is told and his credentials as a seer are established:

## Merlin and the Dragons

Vortigern was the high king of Britain in the days before Arthur. But he gained this position by murdering the rightful king, Constans, and taking his throne by force. Then, driven by fear of reprisals, he employed a force of Saxon mercenaries to protect him. They soon made themselves hated as much as Vortigern himself, and there began among the people of Britain a general uprising. They sent word to the sons of King Constans, who were living in exile in Gaul, to return and crush the usurper.

When news of a great army led by the two princes reached him, Vortigern fled to the mountainous regions of Wales and commanded a strong tower to be built from which he could defend himself against his enemies.

So work began, but every time they began to build, something happened to stop them. They worked hard all day until the walls were as high as a man. But every night, while the builders slept, the walls mysteriously fell down, and they had to begin all over again every morning.

For three days and three nights they struggled to build the walls; then they went to King Vortigern and told him what had happened. Angry and fearful, Vortigern called his chief wizard to tell him what he should do.

The chief wizard consulted his magic books. Then he walked up and down and around and around the ruined walls. At last he stopped by a certain huge boulder and said: "There is only one thing to do. You must find a child that never had a father and kill him on this spot. That will make your castle stand."

Vortigern sent his best men to look for a child who never had a father. They rode all day and all night and all the next day until they came to a town called Carmarthen. There, as they rode along the street, they saw some boys fighting and heard one say to the other: "You never had a father!"

**Merlin**
Alan Lee's powerful modern portrait of Merlin shows him as a shaman and wildman, lost amid the haunted trees of the forest.

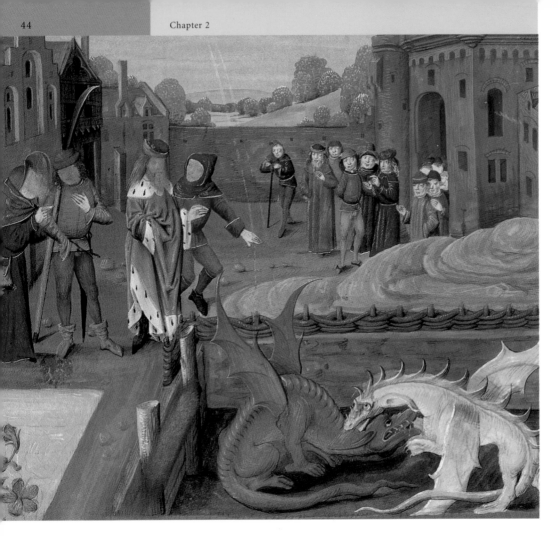

**The Two Dragons**

Merlin reveals the mystery of the two dragons to King Vortigern.

The soldiers took the boy who never had a father, whose name was Emrys, and they rode with him for a night and a day and another night until they reached the place where Vortigern was encamped.

"Here is the child that never had a father," they said.

Vortigern was sitting in his Royal Chair, which he had carried everywhere he went. He looked at the boy, and the boy looked at him.

"I know what you want with me," said Emrys.

"What do you mean?" said Vortigern.

"You want to kill me so that your castle will stand," said the boy.

Vortigern called his chief wizard. "This is the boy that never had a father," he said.

The chief wizard looked at Emrys, and Emrys looked at the chief wizard.

"I know the real reason why the walls won't stand," said the boy.

"Is that so?" said the chief wizard.

"I'll prove it, if you like," said Emrys.

"Go ahead," said the chief wizard, looking at Vortigern to make sure the king agreed. Vortigern nodded.

Everyone looked at the boy who never had a father. A crowd began to gather.

"Under the hill there is a lake full of dark water," said the boy. "That's the first reason why the walls won't stand."

Vortigern ordered his men to dig. Sure enough, when they had dug a deep hole they found a pool of dark water.

Emrys smiled. "At the bottom of the pool is a stone box. That is the second reason why the walls won't stand."

Vortigern's men dug a trench so that the water would drain away. At the bottom of the pool, just as the boy had said, was a huge stone box.

"Inside the box are two dragons," said Emrys. "One of them is red and the other white. All day they sleep, but at night they wake up and fight. Their fighting shakes the earth and causes the walls to fall. That's the third reason."

Vortigern ordered the box to be opened, and out flew the two dragons, who began to fight. At first the red dragon proved to be the stronger, then the white dragon fought back. But in the end it was the red dragon who triumphed, and the white dragon fell dead.

Then the boy Emrys turned to Vortigern and the chief wizard. And there in front of the whole crowd of people he said: "Everything I have told you is the truth. And now I tell you something else. You are like the white dragon, King Vortigern, and your enemies are like the red dragon. Soon Aurelius and Uther will be here, and there will be a great battle. In that battle you will be killed, just as the white dragon was. And there is nothing you can do about it!"

Then Emrys turned around and walked away down the hill, and no one tried to stop him. Everything that he said came true. And the boy grew up to be the wisest man and the most powerful wizard who ever lived. He was no longer called Emrys, but instead people everywhere called him Merlin, and he became King Arthur's closest adviser.

+ + + + +

In the same text from which this story is taken, Merlin prophesies at greater length, relating to events far in the future. Collections of these prophecies were circulating throughout the Middle Ages and they were still being added to as age followed age. This prominent visionary ability remains one of the most essential aspects of the wizards' gifts: enabling them to shape destiny to their own ends, to shine a light into the dark obscurities of the future, and to give valuable insights into times yet to come. Perhaps no other has done this as successfully as the sixteenth-century prophet Nostradamus, whose words have been interpreted for virtually every generation since he first set them down.

# A Positive Future

ichel de Nostredame (1503–1566) is beyond question one of the most famous seers in history, but the methods by which he obtained his visions place him in the class of wizard just as surely as Merlin or the Celtic druids.

Born at St. Remy de Provence to a well-to-do Jewish family, Nostradamus learned Hebrew, Latin, and Greek, and studied kabbala, mathematics, medicine, astrology, and astronomy from an early age, proving to be a brilliant pupil. Then, in 1514, his parents converted to Catholicism and Michel extended his learning even further, adding biblical prophecy and magic to his list of accomplishments.

As a child, he began to experience visions, and this gift continued throughout his life. But in 1522 he went to Montpelier University to study medicine, a skill that his parents hoped would bring both respect and generous financial returns. Once again Michel proved a brilliant scholar, bringing his formidable mind to bear on problems that had occupied the minds of healers for centuries. When he eventually began to practice medicine, he threw out most of the traditional practices of his fellow healers and replaced them with ideas of his own—many far ahead of their time. He also concocted his own medicines, the recipes of which are long since lost but which seem to have produced remarkable results.

Sometime around 1534, Nostradamus settled in Agen, where he married and fathered two children. It was at this time that he met a renowned philosopher and student of astrology named Cesar Scaliger, who appears to have first introduced him to the art of prophecy.

For a time all went well with Nostradamus's life. Then disaster struck when the plague raged through the area and his wife and children died. Shortly after, Nostradamus was summoned to appear before the Inquisition to answer questions concerning possible heretical practices by both Scalier and a mutual friend.

Nostradamus does not seem to have been under suspicion himself, but he chose to leave Agen and for the next six years appears to have wandered across Europe with no particular direction to his life. It was at this time that the visions he had experienced as a child returned to him—though he seemed to do nothing to either test their validity or record them.

**Nostradamus**
Michel de Nostredame was the greatest prophet and seer of the sixteenth century.

**Nostradamus**

Nostradamus's most famous
client was Catherine de Medici.
Here he seeks the answer to
a question for her by casting
a magic spell.

Soon after, he settled down again, this time in Salon en Craux de Provence. There he met and married a wealthy widow named Anne Ponsart Gemelle, who bore him six children. It was at this time, probably around 1550, that he began to systematically record his visions, which now took on a distinctly prophetic color, and which incidentally give us an enlightening glimpse into the practices of this sixteenth-century wizard. Every night he would retire to his study and perform a ritual that consisted of setting up a tripod on which stood a bowl filled with water. Nostradamus would next touch his wand to the tripod, dip it into the water, and touch it to the hem of his robe. He would then sit for hours staring into the bowl, occasionally turning aside to record what he saw. Often he did not understand the things that appeared to him or the messages that were delivered

by a voice inside his head that he called "the divine presence."
Nostradamus soon had a large collection of prophetic
messages, which he had a strong impulse to publish. Knowing
that he risked trial for heresy if he presented his work in
a straightforward manner, he chose to rewrite it in poetic
form. He used rhyming quatrains set forth in a mixture of
Greek, French, Provençal, and Latin. Some words were further
disguised as anagrams, making them even harder to
understand. He published an initial collection of these verses,
which he called *centuries*, in 1555 under the title *Les Prophecies
de M. Michel Nostradamus*. They became an immediate
commercial success and all the rage at the courts of Europe.
No lesser person than Catherine de Medici sought him out,
thus firmly establishing his reputation.

After his death, Nostradamus's works became even
more famous and have continued to this day to be read and
interpreted with a variety of meanings. Among the many
things he is believed to have accurately foretold are the
Napoleonic Wars, the history of the British monarchy from
Elizabeth I to Elizabeth II, the American Revolution and Civil
War, and the rise of Hitler's Third Reich. Some commentators
have found references to the assassinations of both John F.
and Robert Kennedy, as well as the rise of Ayatollah Khomeini
and President Saddam Hussein, and the death of Diana,
Princess of Wales. Most recently, references have been
discovered that apparently indicate that Nostradamus foresaw the destruction of
the Twin Towers on September 11, 2001.

Like those of many other seers and prophets, Nostradamus's writings have
been open to interpretation by each succeeding generation, who in each case
have found meanings appropriate to their own time.

In a letter to his youngest son, Nostradamus said that his prophecies
extended to the year 3797, when the world as we know it will end. He also said
that after a lengthy period of war and strife the world would enter a new golden
age. He believed in the possibility, as stated in the 1558 edition of his work, that
future events could be altered, and one of the reasons why he had sought to
record his visions was to enable men of good conscience to avoid the dangers
that lay ahead. That this has not been the case is clear enough in our own time.
Nevertheless, seers such as Nostradamus showed a side of the wizard's character
that is every bit as important as any of those discussed here—that it was important
to use magical powers to good effect, to help rather than hinder the progress of
human evolution. Nostradamus wanted his prophecies to make the future
a better place and, like many a wizard before him, believed this made magic
a positive influence in the world.

**Nostradamus**
Nostradamus studied the
movements of the stars and
planets to discover future events.

# The Brahan Seer

Not all seers were as universal as Nostradamus, and some sought to use their gift for personal gain. One such was Kenneth Odran, also known by his Gaelic name, Coinneach Odhar Fiosaiche, and as Sallow Kenneth or "the One Who Knows." He was born some time during the latter part of the seventeenth century on the Isle of Lewis off the western coast of Scotland. He had a reputation not only as a great prophet but also as a selfish man who was not averse to taking spiteful vengeance on those he did not like.

The story of his birth marks the entry of a remarkable wizard into the world.

## The Birth of a Seer

One night when she was herding cattle near the graveyard of the church of Baile-na-Cille, a young shepherdess saw a number of ghosts leaving their graves and flying off in various directions. Intrigued as much as fearful, the girl waited and watched, and in time saw the ghostly folk returning. Soon all the graves were filled again, save one. The girl crept nearer and, remembering that rowan was a wood that no spirit could cross, she laid her distaff, which was made of that wood, across the gaping hole in the earth. Not long after that the last ghost came hastening back but found the way barred by the rowan staff. Seeing the girl crouching near, the ghost begged her to remove the distaff.

"First tell me who you are," asked the girl.

"I was the daughter of the king of Norway," answered the ghost. "I drowned in the sea long ago and was buried here."

She went on to explain that every year on this night the ghosts were permitted to visit their old homes. Hers being the farthest away, she was always late to return. "Soon the cock will crow," she said, "and I shall be lost forever. Let me go back into my grave peacefully and I will reward you."

The girl agreed and the ghost took a stone that hung around her own neck and gave it to her. "You will have a son," she prophesied. "When he is seven years old give this stone to him. He will become a great seer and a mighty magician." Then she was gone.

All came to pass as the ghost had foretold. Kenneth's mother gave the stone to him when he was seven. At once he looked through it and saw a beached whale hidden in a bay not too far away—a veritable treasury of food and other supplies for the poor farming community.

✦ ✦ ✦ ✦ ✦ ✦

**Castlerigg**

Castlerigg stone circle in Cumberland, England, is considered one of the most powerful magical sites in Britain.

After this, stories of young Kenneth's abilities spread far and wide. Highland chieftains sought him out, and he became especially linked with the family of the earl of Seaforth, lord of Lewis and most of Rothshire during the second half of the seventeenth century. Lord Seaforth took a liking to the outspoken youth, who could look deeply into the future and was seldom wrong in his predictions.

As his fame spread, an enthusiastic antiquarian from Inverness persuaded the young seer to visit him so that he might record his prophecies. All went well for a time until Kenneth told him that ships would one day pass behind Tomnahurich Hill in Inverness. At this the scholar threw up his hands and decided to write no more since the boy was clearly mad. However, years later, in 1822, the Caledonian Canal was opened and ships did indeed sail where Kenneth had predicted they would.

Fame and success seem to have gone to the young man's head, as he lost no opportunity to speak ill of the landed gentry of the highlands and islands. This made him popular among the poorer folk, who dared not speak out openly against their masters. Despite this, however, Lord Seaforth continued to patronize Kenneth, giving him employment in the castle of Brahan.

Then the day came when Charles II sent his lordship to Paris on an affair of state. Time passed and he did not return. Finally the earl's wife summoned Kenneth, although she did not like him and believed him to be a fraud. She demanded that he look into his stone and tell her the fate of her husband. Kenneth did so and told her with a laugh that she need have no fear for her lord. Suspicious at Kenneth's amused expression, Lady Seaforth pressed him to tell her more. Reluctantly he did so, explaining that he had seen Lord Seaforth in a splendid room in Paris attending upon a beautiful lady. He seemed to expect a reward for this, but Lady Seaforth grew angrier by the minute and ordered Kenneth to be arrested.

At first amazed and then finally realizing that his life was in danger, Kenneth raised his seeing stone to his eye and gave forth the following long and terrible prophecy of the Seaforth family:

> *I see into the far future. I read the doom of my oppressor. The long descended line of Seaforth will, ere many generations have passed, end in extinction and sorrow. I see a chief, the last of his house, both deaf and dumb. He will be father to four fair sons, all of whom will go before him to the tomb. He will live careworn and die mourning, knowing that the honors of his line are to be extinguished forever and that no future chief of Mackenzies will rule at Brahan or Kintail. After lamenting the last and most promising of his sons, he shall sink into the grave, and the remnant of his possessions shall be inherited by a white-hooded widow from the East, and she is to kill her sister.*

**Ravens**

Ravens were considered prophetic by the Celts, their appearance often presaging war or death.

Much of this came true, and the Seaforth family perished within a few generations.

Taken in chains to Chanonry castle, Kenneth was hastily tried and found guilty of witchcraft. He was sentenced to a terrible death—to be thrown head first into a barrel filled with flaming tar through which spikes were stuck. On the way to his death the countess taunted him with assurances that he would never go to heaven. Kenneth replied that he certainly would, since he was innocent, but that the lady would just as assuredly not. "You will see a sign of what I say," he declared. "After my death two birds, a raven and a dove, will circle the sky above my ashes. If the raven alights first, your words will be true; if the dove, then I shall be proved right."

Meanwhile, the earl heard of Kenneth's fate. He hastened home without pausing to rest or eat, killing a horse beneath him and running the last miles. But he was too late. By the time he reached Chanonry, Kenneth was already dying. The earl cried out that he had tried to save him, and the seer replied with a last prophecy: "For what your lady has done this day, your line shall end just as mine begins. After I am dead, a child of my seed shall be born on Brahan land and shall be called the Brahan Child. In each generation thereafter, there shall be one such child, and each shall have the sight that I have had. Let those beware who would seek to harm them, for my shade shall watch over them."

With this, Kenneth spoke no more. The truth of this final prophecy remains unknown, though there are those who have claimed to be descended from the Brahan Seer over the centuries. The fate of Kenneth's seeing stone also remains unknown. It is said that he threw it into Loch Ussie on the way to his trial, while others claim that it fell from his hand and was trampled into the mud of Brahan castle. Whatever the truth, it is a perfect example of the kind of device so often pictured as part of the wizard's equipment, from Dr. Dee's black mirror to the Palantir of Tolkien's *The Lord of the Rings*.

The role of the wizard has always included aspects of the role of the prophet, the one who has the ear of God. The shamans were the first to visit the inner worlds in a trance, stare, and return with information. Skilled seers like Moses, Nostradamus, and the Brahan Seer had the gift of seeing light where others saw darkness. This ability was central to the accomplishment of their tasks and has been an integral aspect of the wizard's abilities ever since.

✦ ✦ ✦ ✦ ✦ ✦

# Divination and Vision

The ability of the wizard to divine answers to specific questions is an essential skill. Contrary to a widely held belief, divination is not the art of foretelling the future but a method for taking soundings among the many possibilities for the future. The wizard seeks an answer by being in the moment, the now, and seeking to divine, from the consciousness of the universe, an answer that will be as true as possible. Two ways of working with the natural world as a basis for divination, both based on very ancient techniques, follow here. Both are perfectly safe and require no special abilities beyond the simple belief in the possibility of seeing more deeply than our common state of awareness.

# READING THE CLOUDS

The technique that follows comes from the ancient Celts. In more than one ancient text we read of those who practiced the divinatory skill of *neldoracht*, cloud watching. It was the task of these people to seek answers to specific questions by observing the shape and disposition of clouds. This is easy enough to do in most parts of the world and requires only a basic understanding of the forces involved.

When you look up at the sky you will often see clouds, and most of us at some time or another have engaged in the activity of seeing shapes there. But what if this is seen not as a means of idling away the time on a warm summer day but as a way of discovering answers to questions?

## HERE IS HOW IT WORKS:

First, of course, you need a day in which the sky is clear and cloudy—when the sky is sufficiently clear to define the shapes of the clouds. If there is a wind to keep them moving, so much the better. Next, and most important, you need to have a question or an issue, a purpose for making your divination. Ask about something that you've not been able to resolve or find help for. Don't ask for frivolous things to test the oracle. Treat it with respect and you will receive a response you can respect in turn! Getting the question right—finding the right words to use—is every bit as important as looking for the answer. Thus, it is good to avoid either/or questions such as: "Should I marry Jim or Bill?" The kinds of questions that work best are those in which the questioner is looking for a defining answer rather than an exact or irrevocable sign. Thus, to follow the example given here, another way to approach the issue would be: "Please give me helpful guidance about marrying Jim/Bill." This opens up the entire application and makes the response more likely to be accurate and helpful.

Clearly indicate that you are starting your divination by asking your question aloud. Then lie down on the ground and look up at the clouds. Some of the ancient diviners used to look into a still lake or a pool of water caught in a hollowed-out stone. This may still be done today by simply filling a bowl with water and looking at the sky reflected in it. This also has the advantage of limiting the area of sky to be "read." Whichever method you decide to use, close your eyes for a moment and consider your question as deeply as possible. Try to clear your mind of all distracting thoughts. When you feel ready, open your eyes and scan the sky for cloud forms. It's really important that you do not try to force the shapes you see to fit the question. Sometimes the clouds will seem to offer up shapes that have nothing at all to do with your query. Yet one of the greatest secrets of any form of divination is to remain open to the possibility that the patterns you seek will be entirely different from what you expect.

Suppose your request is: "I am considering changing my job; please show me the way forward." Then, when you look up at the clouds, you see something that looks like an open mouth. What do you think this means? Could it be that if you change your job you will be swallowed up? What if you look just a little obliquely? Maybe you can see the mouth as your own, gulping down the new opportunities offered by changing your life. Could it be that you are hungry for change? What do you feel? What memories and images come to you as you gaze at the clouds?

When the signs are open to more than one interpretation, it is wise to look again. What other cloud shapes are in the sky at this moment? Can you see something that looks like a pair of scissors or a knife? Could this mean that you should cut your ties with your current place of work? It is critically important to get the question right because multiple explanations may occur to you.

If the question is too vague, go deeper and refine it. A better way of wording the request might be: "Show me how I will be better off if I change my job." Now the pattern is clearer. Look again and see what further sights are there. In what direction are they in relation to you?

Are they low on the horizon or high? If there is more than one shape that seems significant, how do they lie in relation to each other? What kind of clouds are they? Are they thick, thin, wispy, heavy, full of rain (and, if so, is the rain ominous or much needed?)? Are they lit above or below by the sun? All of these things can be seen as part of the pattern and can help to refine the answer you seek.

By being sensitive to the moment you can gradually define the reading until it becomes clear. And you can do this over and over again. If you feel you did not receive an answer from the first reading, wait awhile and then try again, always being careful to phrase the question as exactly as possible.

When you have finished, clearly mark that you are finished by thanking the oracle-clouds and taking a few moments of quietness to consider the answers you may have received and to make any notes that seem appropriate.

With time, you will find that you become quite adept at reading the patterns in the cloud, and that the merest glance will tell you what you need to know. As with any method of divination, it is important to remember that these are only indicators. Do not look for the meaning of everything in the clouds (or anywhere else, for that matter), and try not to read too much into what you see. All such methods are intended to offer only pointers, to add guidance to decisions we have to take, or questions to which we need answers. They are not intended to be irrevocable statements of what will happen. Any proficient seer or diviner will always preface a prophetic statement by indicating that this is one possibility only, one answer among many. To take what you read in the sky as a foolproof exemplar is an unwise course of action.

Try the oracle's advice and see what happens. Review what the results have been at the end of a designated time—a week or month. How have things developed? If the sign has been helpful, you will begin to build confidence and learn how to read what the clouds are showing you with better understanding. Interpretation will grow easier.

# READING THE STONES

The Navahos of the American Southwest practice a fascinating form of divination that is easily used by anyone anywhere. It requires only a stone, of roughly hand size or smaller, that has at least four distinct planes. It doesn't need to be square but needs only to have surfaces that are distinct from each other. The idea is simply that once you have formulated your question, you will sit with this stone for a while and study each surface, examining all the tiny shapes and irregularities, looking for pictures in the stone, noting the differences as well as the similarities between the surfaces. Does one side reflect the other? Does a picture overlap from one side to the next? Feel the stone with your eyes closed to heighten your sense of touch.

In this way you build up a gradual picture that you may then apply to your question. It is essentially the same as with the cloud-watching technique described on pages 55–56. Begin by getting your question right; keep it in mind while you get to know your stone. (Choosing the stone can be part of the task. Whether you are on a beach or a patch of stony earth, let yourself wander, staying alert to the stones until one "speaks" to you.) The entire process should take no more than fifteen to twenty minutes, though you can take as long as you wish. Once you have finished, thank the stone and replace it on the land—whether at the original place where you found it or in another wild spot is up to you. As always, take time to consider the things you observed and how they relate to your question.

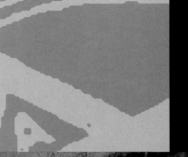

# 3 | Elemental Wizardry

# WHERE EARTH MEETS SKY

The province of the . . . magician
is all things in heaven and earth.

C. GRANT LOOMIS, *WHITE MAGIC*

# THE PILLARS OF THE WORLD

Control over the elements is very much a part of the wizard's gift. Whether we think of Pythagoras's follower Abaris flying through the air on his golden arrow, or Saruman in *The Lord of the Rings* calling up the worst storm in living memory to bring down snow and ice to destroy the Fellowship of the Ring, it is clear that this ability is an important aspect of magical lore. Indeed, magicians and alchemists have sought to master and harmonize the elements since the first shamans walked the earth. As forces in the universe, each element has its part to play. However, different combinations cause different reactions. It is the metaphysical reality behind this that is important to the magician, rather than the physical presence of the elements.

A Polish alchemist named Michael Sendivogius (1566–1633) elaborated on this when he wrote:

> There are four elements, [but] each has at its center another element [or archetype] that makes it what it is. These are the four pillars of the world. They were in the beginning evolved and molded out of chaos by the hand of the Creator; and it is their contrary action that keeps up the harmony and equilibrium of the universe; it is they that, through the virtue of celestial influences, produce all things above and below the earth.

It was thus important for the wizard to understand how the elements worked and how they could be recombined so that their qualities could be altered. Many would have been familiar with Aristotle's belief that the structure of the universe is made up of the elements in various combinations, each of which can be changed by altering its

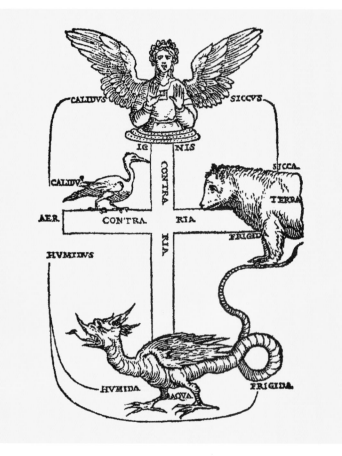

**Pillars of the World**

An alchemical design depicting the four elements as the foundation of the world. The four creatures represent earth, air, fire, and water at each of the quarters, showing the underlying harmony in all things.

basic constituents. We might think of fire as hot and dry, of water as cold and moist, of earth as cold and dry, and of air as moist and hot. However, these aspects can be effectively changed to create subtle variants. If the elements themselves originated by impressing the *prima materia* of the universe with different qualities, then it should be possible to manipulate these to bring about changes within matter. The qualities of cold and moist created water when they were brought together. But by adding heat, this same element is changed into air (steam).

This kind of prescientific discipline was considered to be a magical practice in the Renaissance and earlier. The ability to bring about such changes was central to a wizard's visible skills. In addition, knowledge and understanding of elemental forces were part of his continuing search for a greater degree of harmony with the universe. Thus much time and effort were devoted to understanding elemental constructs, though the effects to be gained varied enormously and were put to many different uses. In the story that follows, the Druidic magic of Mog Ruith is used to call up storms and mists, as well as to move mountains. Later we will see how the Jewish magicians who sought power over the elements exercised their skills to create the golem, an artificial creature made of earth.

# A Druid Battle

One of the greatest of the many Druid magicians of early Ireland was Mog Ruith, whose name literally means "Devotee of the Wheel." He may originally have been a god, but the surviving traditions describe him in more human terms, albeit those of a very powerful human. Interestingly, Mog Ruith was blind, having lost one eye climbing in the Alps and the other while holding back the sun for two days—both actions that give some indication of his strength. However, loss of sight in no way impaired his skills as a magician, as we see in the following story that is adapted from a translation by Caitlín Matthews.

## THE SIEGE OF DRUIM DAMHGAIRE

One day Cormac Mac Art, the king of Ireland, led his army into Munster, determined to exact double the tribute due him from Fiacha, the king of that province. With Cormac were his Druids, who caused all the rivers and streams and wells to dry up so that there was not a drop of water in the entire place. King Fiacha grew desperate. "Who is there in the whole of Ireland who can help us?" he asked of his advisers. With one accord they said that he should summon the druid Mog Ruith, who had acquired wisdom over seven centuries.

So Fiacha sent word to the Druid and asked what payment he would require to save them. Mog Ruith replied that he would need "a hundred bright white cows in milk, a hundred well-fattened pigs, a hundred strong working oxen, a hundred racehorses, fifty soft white cloaks." After he had done what was required of him, he added, "the king of Munster should choose his counselor from among my descendants, and I should be given the territory of my choice in Munster."

To these demands King Fiacha agreed, and soon Mog Ruith arrived. He ordered that two sharp, five-pointed spears be cast in such a way that they stuck in the earth. This caused the waters to flow once again.

Next day Mog Ruith asked, "What help do you need now?"

"Yonder hill has been raised above us by Cormac's Druids," said the king.

"Someone turn my face toward the hill," said Mog Ruith. This was done without hesitation. Immediately he invoked his god and through his power grew so tall that he was scarcely less high than the hill, the sight of which brought terror to all who looked upon him. Then Mog Ruith began to blow upon the hill. The attacking warriors were unable to stay in their tents, so great was the storm. Cormac's Druids did not know the cause of the great wind. Finally, the hill disappeared altogether in dark clouds and a whirlwind of fog. All that could be heard were the cries of confusion from the shattered army resounding on all sides as the hill was reduced to its foundations.

Shaken by this display, Cormac sent his chief druid, Colphtha, into the fight. Mog Ruith, informed of his coming, told his pupil, Cennmar, to prepare for battle, requesting that he give him his poisoned stone. This was done, and he began to praise it and put upon it a venomous charm.

Then he gave the stone back to Cennmar and sent him against Colphtha. And as they fought Mog Ruith caused stones and sand to become firebrands so that Colphtha was sorely burned. And in addition he made all the cows, bulls, ants, boars, and even the plants that grew there to cry out against his enemy. Colphtha saw Mog Ruith across the ford and realized who had made these enchantments, and he was sore afraid.

Then Mog Ruith said: "Short shall be your existence and the existence of your race." And at this moment, Cennmar placed the charmed hand-stone in the ford's waters. There it became a giant conger eel, while Cennmar himself turned to stone. Then Colphtha and the eel fought, and the creature broke the Druid's arms and tied itself in nine knots about him, sinking its teeth into his head. Cennmar then transformed himself into his own form again and cast one of the magical lances at Colphtha, who fell dead.

After several more attempts to overcome Mog Ruith, Cormac's Druids decided to light Druidic fires to confound their enemies with dark smoke. When he heard this, Mog Ruith told Fiacha's men to bring handfuls of rowan wood. Fiacha himself was to bring a bundle of wood from the side of a mountain where it had grown, sheltered from the wind of March, the wind of the sea, and the wind that causes forest fires. "The fire is ready," said Cennmar at last. "Now it only needs lighting."

Mog Ruith struck his tinderbox. Then he said to the Munstermen, "Quickly, each shave a sliver of wood from your spear handles." They did so and gave the slivers to him. He then mixed them with butter and laid the ball on the fire, chanting the while:

"I mix a roaring, fierce fire,
Clearing woods, blighting grass,
Angry flame of powerful speed,
Rushing to skies above,
Subduing other fires' wrath,
Making battle on Cormac's race."

Tossed into the fire's heart, the ball lit with a great flame and great uproar that caused Cormac's warriors to retreat.

"Now," said Mog Ruith, "make ready my chariot and hold your horses in readiness also. If the fire turns toward the north, you must be ready to charge. If they come from the north, prepare to defend yourselves."

As he said this, he sent a Druidic wind into the atmosphere, so that it formed itself into a dark and shadowy cloud from which a rain of blood fell. And Mog Ruith sang:

"I send a spell with the aid of a cloud.

A rain of blood upon the grass."

Then Mog Ruith asked for his brown hornless bull's hide and his bird headdress that was decorated with flying wings. And with these he rose into the heavens and started to beat the air, so as to turn the fires toward the north, all the time chanting spells.

Soon enough the flames turned northward, and Mog Ruith descended and mounted upon his chariot. He sent Cennmar to urge the Munstermen forward, and all advanced, following the Druid. When he saw this, Cormac conceded defeat to the Munstermen, and with all his men withdrew from the province into his own land again. As for Mog Ruith, he chose the land that he desired from among the lands of King Fiacha and the woman he most wished to be with, and he went to live with her in that place from that time forward.

✦  ✦  ✦  ✦  ✦

This story describes a wizard with awesome power over the elements. His superior abilities clearly derive from the experience he gained over seven centuries of life, many of them spent in the fairy hills. His ability to fly is also an indication of his further power over the air, though he is not alone in Celtic tradition in possessing this skill. Bladud, the legendary king of Bath, who is said to have introduced magical arts into Britain, made a pair of wings for himself. However, he later fell from the Temple of Apollo in London much as Simon Magus fell from the sky when he challenged St. Peter to a flying match.

**Druid battle**

Druids often used the elements to fight their magical battles, as here where the very ground burns beneath the trees.

# A Dark Dichotomy

The wizard's control over the elements draws attention to another theme that lies at the heart of his world—the struggle between light and dark, good and evil, positive and negative. The questions that remain at the heart of all magic are the same as those asked again and again of nature and the elements: Are they good or evil? Personal or impersonal? Is the lightning bolt that strikes the tree and kills the man sitting beneath it an expression of God's anger or a natural event over which we have no control? When wizards sought just such control over the elements—as in the case of Moses parting the Red Sea or Mog Ruith calling up a Druidic mist—were they performing an evil action or simply harnessing a natural power to augment their own abilities? Such questions are constantly asked throughout the lives of the great magicians of the Renaissance. Of all these, one in particular stands out as the most archetypal, deeply flawed, and splendid wizard of all time—although he is fictitious.

The story of Prospero is told in Shakespeare's play *The Tempest*, which is dated to 1612. He embodies virtually all the characteristics of the wizard. He is wily, powerful, and secretive. He also has access to great power—particularly over the elements. *The Tempest* is one of Shakespeare's most powerful and moving works largely because of the ambivalence of its central character. Prospero, like most dramatic representations of the wizard during the Renaissance, represents the paradox at the heart of all who sought to enter the dangerous backwaters of magic. They were men who had found their way to virtually limitless power but who were constrained by the limitations of moral behavior and humanistic beliefs. Thus, while it was permitted (under strong prescriptions of caution) to study magic, it was less allowable to practice it. This dichotomy lies at the heart of every wizard we have studied here, but it is nowhere more clearly stated than in Shakespeare's play and in the character of Prospero.

*Opposite* **Prospero's Books**
The late Sir John Gielgud in the role of Shakespeare's wizard Prospero, from the 1991 Peter Greenaway movie *Prospero's Books*.

# On Prospero's Island

**Caliban**
Caliban, the earthy child of the witch Sycorax, watches over the sleeping Miranda as Prospero prepares to cast a spell over his enemies.

*T*he Tempest opens with the great storm that Prospero has conjured to bring about the shipwreck of the craft carrying Alonso, the king of Naples, his brother, Sebastian, his son, Ferdinand, and Prospero's own brother, Antonio, who had succeeded him as duke of Milan after Prospero had been thrown out for the study and practice of magic. Still smarting from this act of usurpation, Prospero seeks revenge. However, his daughter, Miranda, pleads with him to abate the storm, and this he reluctantly does. This action shows Prospero's power, even though the task is carried out by his elemental spirits.

Shakespeare gives us two memorable portraits of magical allies in Prospero's main helpers. Ariel is a sprite of the air. Caliban is a creature of the earth and the misshapen child of the witch Sycorax, the true ruler of the island where Prospero and Miranda live.

The relationships of these two otherworldly beings to their master are wonderfully developed from accounts common to virtually all wizards. They range from a kind of friendly alliance to bitter slavery, represented in the play by the two spirits. Ariel, rescued from imprisonment in a cloven pine tree by Prospero, serves his master willingly enough:

*All hail, great master, grave sir, hail. I come*
*To answer thy best pleasure. Be't to fly,*
*To swim, to dive into the future, to ride*
*On the curled clouds, to thy strong*
*bidding task*
*Ariel and all his quality. (Act 1, Scene 2)*

Caliban, on the other hand, can think of nothing but ways to have his revenge on the magician and to regain his freedom and the island that is his inheritance.

The different attitudes of Ariel and Caliban really represent the magician's elemental power. Almost every speech they utter in the play has imagery borrowed from the elements themselves. But they are also aspects of Prospero himself—his light and dark selves—as well as being metaphors for the dark and light dichotomy at the heart of all Renaissance magic.

The play is an exploration of this dichotomy. The story is full of the twists and turns, romantic substitutions, and magical tricks so beloved of Shakespeare. But as Prospero seeks to control the fates of the shipwrecked people, he gradually learns to relinquish his controlling desire for revenge and reverts to his former self. As the story unfolds, the spells that bind everyone on the island are all overturned.

Prospero finally rejects magic and returns to the world of the everyday, destroying both his book and his staff. This is not only a personal statement from the greatest dramatist the world has known but also hints at the possible fate of all wizards who seek to depend solely on the path of magic. The great speech in which Prospero abjures magic perfectly sums up the Renaissance imagery of the wizard and his craft.

**Prospero's Island**

In Shakespeare's *The Tempest*, the magical island of the wizard Prospero is guarded by the spirits of earth and air, Caliban and Ariel.

> *Ye elves of hills, brooks, standing lakes, and groves,*
> *And ye that on the sands with printless foot*
> *Do chase the ebbing Neptune, and do fly him*
> *When he comes back; you demi-puppets, that*
> *By moon-shine do the green sour ringlets make,*
> *Whereof the ewe not bites; and you whose pastime*
> *Is to make midnight mushrooms, that rejoice*
> *To hear the solemn curfew, by whose aid*
> *(Weak masters tho' ye be) I have be-dimm'd*
> *The noon-tide sun, called forth the mutinous winds,*
> *And 'twixt the green sea and the azur'd vault*
> *Set roaring war to the dread rattling thunder*
> *Have I giv'n fire, and rifted Jove's stout oak*
> *With his own bolt; the strong-bas'd promontory*
> *Have I made shake, and by the spurs pluck'd up*
> *The pine and cedar: graves at my command*
> *Have wak'd their sleepers; op'd, and let 'em forth*
> *By my so potent art. But this rough magic*
> *I here abjure; and when I have requir'd*
> *Some heav'nly music, which ev'n now I do,*
> *(To work mine end upon their senses that*
> *This airy charm is for) I'll break my staff,*
> *Bury it certain fathoms in the earth,*
> *And deeper than did ever plummet sound,*
> *I'll drown my book. (Act 5, Scene 1)*

# Men of Mud

**Golem**

A matchbox cover from present-day Prague shows that the golem is still remembered in the city.

The wizard's control over the elements resulted in some strange side effects. One of these is the creation of the homunculus, a being of clay created from the stuff of earth and animated by the breath of air. Simon Magus, the protowizard of ancient Rome, claimed to have created a child in typically vaunting style, by "turning air into water, and water again into blood, and solidifying it into flesh . . . a much nobler work than that of God the Creator. For He created a man from the earth, but I from the air—a far more difficult matter."

The earliest references to creations of this kind are the tales of statues that came to life, through the agency either of a wizard or of the gods. In classical Greece we hear of several "living" statues, such as the two women, one called Veritas (Truth) and the other Mendacio (Lie), who were created, respectively, by the sculptor Promotes and his apprentice. Both became living creatures after the gods intervened. The most famous story of this kind concerns the punishment meted out to humanity after the Titan Prometheus stole fire from the gods for mankind. Zeus made a woman from clay, whom he named Pandora (all-giving), and gifted her with such curiosity that she later opened a vessel containing all the ills and evils of the world, thus letting them loose forever.

But it is in Jewish tradition that we hear of the deliberate creation of creatures from the earth by human beings rather than a god. One legend tells how Enoch, a grandson of Adam, was asked to demonstrate how God brought about the first creation of man. Enoch took dust and water, mixed them into mud, and shaped them into a man—the first golem. He then blew life into the nostrils of his creation, but Satan found a way into this unholy object and it became the center of a cult and later had to be destroyed.

Elsewhere we hear of the golem, a creature wholly made of earth. Its history brings us in contact with some unusual magicians—the rabbis of Central Europe. The word *golem*, which literally means "body without soul," clearly separates the artificial creature from a living, breathing human being. The word actually appears only once in the Hebrew Bible (Psalms 139:16), where the reference is to the creation of Adam. But there have been numerous interpretations of this reference through the centuries, and in talmudic literature the golem is referred to as a stage of the creation of the first man. According to this tradition God took twelve hours to complete Adam, making a number of failed attempts in the process, one of which was the golem.

**Golem**

Harry Bauer as Emperor Rudolf II chaining up the golem played by Ferdinand Hart in the eponymous 1936 silent movie *The Golem*.

A later tradition refers to a magical book, the *Sefer Yetzira*, which dates from late antiquity and is not unlike the later grimoires of medieval Europe. This book described the letters of the Hebrew alphabet as the building blocks of creation and taught that they could be manipulated in a way that gave those who worked with them unlimited power. If, as the book suggested, God created human beings from the power of letters, then it must also be possible for us to create a being in the same way. Of course, the exact formula required could be learned only through years of mystical discipline and study. That is why it is invariably the rabbis who are described as seeking out the answer to this mystery and thus being responsible for the golem.

One group in particular, the Pietists, who flourished in Germany throughout the twelfth and thirteenth centuries, were believed to have created more than one golem. The main figures in the movement, Rabbi Samuel and

Rabbi Judah, were believed to have been especially successful. The writings of one of their followers, Eleazar of Worms, remains the best source of golem recipes. These recipes show, however, that the rabbis who created the golem were not working with straightforward magic. Rather, it is clear that the creatures were somehow brought into being as part of a mystical or ecstatic state of consciousness, and they existed only while this state of being lasted.

But these beings could be troublesome. A Polish rabbi named Jaffe created a golem to light fires for him on the Sabbath. But the creature went out of control one day and set fire to everything in sight. A later rabbi named Elijah of Chelm, a famous sixteenth-century healer and magician, made a golem to be his servant. At first all went well, but gradually the creature grew so strong and difficult to control that Rabbi Elijah had to destroy it. Interestingly, this was done by removing a card hung around its neck on which was written the sacred word of creation, the aleph. Once this was done the creature returned to dust at once.

This story is similar to those that describe the reanimation of mummies, who were brought back to life by having a text from the Egyptian *Book of the Dead* placed in their mouths. This tradition, alongside the Jewish one, reflects a belief in the power of language itself, of words that could, if properly learned and spoken, bring about miraculous events. This is the most likely origin for the many different words of power used by wizards down the ages to cause changes.

The best-known golem legends originate around the sixteenth century in the city of Prague. Rabbi Judah Low (c. 1525–1609) was the greatest Judaic scholar and mystic of his time. But he was eventually excommunicated in the belief that he had not only practiced forbidden magic but also created a golem according to the ancient methods described in the *Sefer Yetzira*. He did this to protect the ghettos of Prague, which were under threat of persecution at that time. The golem became a deterrent to all who sought to persecute the Jews of the city. Only when the danger was passed did Rabbi Low take the creature to the attic of the Altneuschul, the ancient synagogue of Prague, where he removed the paper bearing the sacred name just as Rabbi Elijah had done. At this point the golem fell to dust. This same dust is said to be preserved to this day in the closed attic of the synagogue, though it is many years since the golem last walked the streets of the city.

All these tales of the making of homunculi follow on one of the first and oldest themes in the history of the wizard—what happens when he seeks too much power. By creating a living being from the elements, a human is seeking to imitate God. In each case where the golem is created to serve its master in a moral cause, as in the case of Rabbi Low, it is permitted to exist for a time; however, when the use to which it is put is purely selfish or motivated by greed, as in the instance of Rabbi Elijah of Chelm, the golem turns into a monster.

**Prague**

The golem was said to haunt the ghettos of Prague in times of danger. Some of the dust from which it was formed is believed to be still hidden in the attic of a synagogue in the city.

# ELEMENTAL BATTLERS

The Finnish Vainamoinen had especially powerful connections with the elements. He was a godlike cultural hero with elements of the trickster and the magician in his character. His mother was a daughter of the air, and he himself was born in water, over which he had a special power throughout his life. His life began with a sixty-year gestation. Eventually he had to break free, falling from his mother's womb into the sea. From there he made his way to land and became the first man to till the soil. This attracted the envy of a Laplander named Joukahainen, who challenged his power. In the ensuing magical contest, Vainamoinen displayed his phenomenal power over the elements by causing mountains to tremble and rocks to split into slivers. He also changed his adversary's possessions into various natural objects. Thus Joukahainen's sleigh became a lake, his whip a reed, and his horse a river. Not yet content, Vainamoinen then turned the challenger's bow into a rainbow, his sword into a bolt of lightning, his dog into a rock, and his clothes into clouds and water lilies. Finally admitting defeat, Joukahainen offered Vainamoinen his sister in marriage. But she jumped into the sea rather than marry Vainamoinen, who had the appearance of an old man.

**Vainamoinen**
Vainamoinen, hero of the Finnish folk epic *The Kalevala*, was a wizard who had immense power over the elements.

Vainamoinen asked his mother's help in seeking a wife, and she, speaking from the bottom of the sea, advised him to seek a woman from the northern land of Pohjola. There followed an extraordinary series of adventures, each of which illustrates Vainamoinen's power over the elements.

# VAINAMOINEN'S QUEST

Vainamoinen loved the Maid of Pohja, but she would not marry him unless he carried out certain tasks. First, she wanted him to split a horsehair with a blunt knife. Then she asked that he tie a knot in an egg, peel a stone, and cut a block of ice without creating any splinters. Finally, she asked him to carve a boat from pieces of her spindle and shuttle. All of these things wise Vainamoinen carried out, except for the last. While he was busy carving the keel of the boat, his axe slipped and buried itself in his knee. Unable to remember the spell that would remove it, Vainamoinen asked a local wise man, who healed him.

Having failed in the tasks set him by the Maid of Pohja, Vainamoinen returned home. But he could not get the woman out of his mind, and so he decided to build another ship to carry him back to Pohjola. For long months he labored over the craft, saying all the right spells over it. All was going well until it came to the last spell, the one that would bind the timbers together and make them watertight. Then Vainamoinen discovered that he had forgotten part of the spell—the last three words he needed escaped him no matter how hard he thought.

So Vainamoinen decided that he must go the Underworld of Tuonela to find the missing words. He set out at once and walked for three weeks. The first week he walked through shrub land, the second through woodland, and the third through thick forest. At last he came to the great black river that guarded the entrance to Tuonela, and there he saw two hideous daughters of Tuoni and Tuoneta, who ruled over the Underworld. Vainamoinen used all his skills and wiles to persuade them to carry him across the river, but when he was at last in the Underworld Tuonela they told him that he would never leave there alive. Then Tuoni commanded his son to enclose Vainamoinen in a net of steel and imprison him at the bottom of the river. But once he had rested, the wily wizard took on the shape of a serpent and escaped through the mesh of the net. Then he regained the bank of the river that lay in the real world and set off again in search of the lost words from his spell.

On the way he met an ancient shepherd, who advised him to seek out the terrible giant Vipunen, who lay under the skin of the earth and from whose body grew certain magical trees. These Vainamoinen cut down: the poplar that grew from the giant's shoulders, the birch that grew from his temples, the fir from his forehead, the alder from his cheeks, and the wild pine tree from his teeth. At the moment when he felt the giant begin to stir, shaking the earth, Vainamoinen thrust his iron-shod staff into the giant's throat. The giant woke fully, gagging on the staff, and with a great breath drew Vainamoinen into his mouth and swallowed him whole. Once inside the giant's belly the wily magician made an anvil from one of his knees and a hammer from his elbow. Then he turned his shirt into a forge and his coat into a pair of bellows and began to heat up a fire.

Soon it got so hot and the blows on the anvil made the giant's heart ache so much that he regurgitated Vainamoinen and reluctantly told him the three words that would complete his spell over the boat.

After all his adventures Vainamoinen set sail again for Pohjola to woo the Maid, but his brother Ilmarinen had got there first and had married her. So upset was Vainamoinen that he decided to steal the most precious thing in that land, the Sampo, a miraculous vessel that had untold powers. Sailing in his magical ship, Vainamoinen carried off the sacred treasure after first singing a magical song that put everyone in the land into a deep sleep. But as he was departing one of the sailors sang a loud song of triumph, which awoke the people of Pohjola. Louhi, the queen of that land, raised a terrible storm, and Vainamoinen only just escaped with his life.

As for the Sampo, it was broken and most of the fragments fell into the sea. But Vainamoinen managed to save enough of them to make a deal with Louhi, who used her magic to turn the land of Kalevala into a fair and prosperous place, full of game and running with swift streams. Because of this, Vainamoinen became a great hero to his people and is remembered still as the greatest magician ever to live in the far northern lands.

✦ ✦ ✦ ✦

**Vainamoinen**
The mighty Finnish wizard Vainamoinen, as portrayed in a painting by the nineteenth-century artist Akseli Gallen-Kallela.

It is through the magical use of words and songs that Vainamoinen exercises control over the elements, just as the golem could be animated only by the sacred word of God. It is Vainamoinen's forgetfulness—his inability to recover the right words—that sends him forth on this adventure. He is, in many ways, the most godlike of all the characters discussed in this book. Yet despite this he is flawed and human in a way that makes him a recognizably heroic figure who just happens to be well versed in magic.

All of the wizards discussed here had power of a particular kind over the elements. Once again we see a central theme in the history of wizardry: It is the use or misuse to which such powers are put that determines the ultimate fate of the wizard. When wizards are concerned to follow the precepts of the Emerald Tablet, they are successful. But some, like Prospero, demonstrate that such powers are not to be used lightly. They can easily change the one who wields them, and not always for the better. But wizards are not a breed to be easily turned aside from such difficult paths. Most will triumph over this treacherous aspect of their powers—though some, as we shall see in the next chapter, fall by the wayside.

# WORKING WITH THE ELEMENTS

The power of the elements has been recognized since the beginning of time. Among many magical orders, learning to work with earth, air, fire, and water is an essential part of the wizard's training. This also has a great deal to do with magical orientation: learning to recognize, instinctively, the directions of the magical compass and the associations with them. A simple diagram shows how the elements are arranged according to the cardinal points of the compass. In addition, there are associations with both the direction and the element that add to the orientation. The purpose of this diagram is to show you how you can invoke one of the many helpful spirits linked with the elements and their associated qualities:

EARTH
**gnomes**
*stability • wisdom*
*clarity of thought • endurance*
*winter*

WATER
**undines**
*emotion • fertility*
*love • compassion*
*tides of the moon*
*twilight*
*fall*

AIR
**sylphes**
*renewal of life*
*birth • inspiration*
*germination*
*spring*

FIRE
**salamanders**
*light • strength*
*humanity • changing direction*
*summer*

I If you require the help of a spirit of air to further your creative life, for example, you might invoke the power of the sylphes, by facing east. With eyes closed, and focusing your will and intention as powerfully as possible, say something like:

*Powers of Air I call upon you!*
*Put me in touch with my creative self*
*As deeply as possible.*
*Awaken within me*
*The energies of creativity.*
*Direct my path to the heart of creation.*

2 If, at some other time, you required help from the watery undines—perhaps to strengthen your emotional life—you could stand facing west, calling upon the powers of that direction thus:

*Powers of Water I call upon you!*
*Help me to find my emotional self*
*As completely as possible.*
*Let me drink*
*From the fountains of pure feeling,*
*Guide my steps to the gates of life.*

3 Again, supposing you needed help with luck—as we often do. In this instance, you would invoke the power of earth, which is associated with this aspect of life, and the power of the gnomes. Here you should face north and call upon them as follows:

*Powers of Earth I call upon you!*
*Help me find my luck.*
*Guide my steps to the path*
*Of great good fortune,*
*Gather the qualities I most require*
*To find the path I need to take.*

4 Finally, if you need to improve your general state of health (always remembering that this is not a substitute for medical treatment), you should look to the south and the power of fire and the salamanders, using words resembling the following:

*Powers of Fire I call upon you!*
*Restore my health,*
*Strengthen my vitality.*
*Awaken a fire within me,*
*Bring me to the doors of life,*
*Reestablish my connection with the joy of being.*

The action of standing, facing the direction, and calling upon the power of the element is far more profound than you may think. Knowing which direction to face, what spirit or element to invoke, and what help is likely to be forthcoming makes your request all the more exact. As you do this you are standing in a place where wizards have stood for thousands of years, uttering formulas (whatever words you choose) that have acted for them though the ages. This alone is a powerfully magical act. Coupled with your will and intention, it brings greater results.

Once you get used to working in this way, other connections will arise that you will want to add. Try redrawing the basic diagram and pinning it up on the wall. Add things as they occur to you. Try to memorize them so that when the need arises you will know instinctively which direction to turn to and which power to invoke.

This is one of the basic principles of all magical work. As such, it opens the door to all kinds of further training in the way of the wizard and also creates within you a profound awareness of the elemental world that is everywhere around you.

**Dr. Faust**
According to legend, the wizard
Dr. Faust obtained his magical
powers by entering into a pact
with the devil.

4 | Wizards Light and Dark

# The Dark Brotherhood

Who in his own skill confiding
Shall with rule and line
Mark the border-land dividing
Human and Divine.

HENRY WADSWORTH LONGFELLOW, *"HERMES TRISMEGISTUS"*

## Good Versus Evil

Are wizards good or evil? This question has vexed the minds of people for almost as long as wizards have been around. Some would state, unequivocally, that they are evil; others, that they are good; while a third group would claim that most wizards occupy a gray area between light and dark. In all probability it is the last group that is nearest the truth. Some wizards, such as Gilles de Rais, Simon Magus, or Gerbert of Aurillac, have a reputation for being entirely evil, and their actions seem to support this. Others, such as Merlin, King Solomon, and Roger Bacon, seem to do only good with their power, or are at worst given to playing tricks, some of which are cruel and others not. A third group, among whom are Faust and the Scottish wizard Michael Scot, seem to waver between black and white. The truth of the matter is that, as with power itself, there is really no simple black and white. Wizards may use their power for good or evil and are credited accordingly. Christianity had a simple standard for judgment: Did the wizard follow the will of God or attempt to follow a personal will? There is a fine line dividing these two states, and crossing over the border has caused many wizards to be portrayed as evil. They do not necessarily perform acts of evil, but they dare, as the American poet Henry Wadsworth Longfellow wrote in the poem quoted above, to "mark the border-land dividing human and divine."

God and devil, angel and demon, good wizard and evil, are polarized sets of images in our consciousness to this day. This same duality is often expressed within our own lives. We too may demonstrate darker urges alongside those of the light. However, the wizard seldom talks about *good* and *evil* because these terms are

**The Wizard**

Merlin teaches his magic to the faery Vivienne in this late nineteenth-century painting by Sir Edward Burne-Jones.

qualitative and misleading, and what may be good to one person can seem evil to another. Instead, the wizard seeks to see things in terms of more balanced polarities. This is not to say that for magicians there is no expression of good and evil in life—they know very well that there is—but that it is preferable not to see these concepts in terms of absolute realities.

The truly great wizards strive to follow the precepts laid down long ago—to perfect themselves and the world around them, to bring harmony where there is strife, to balance the unbalanced.

Evil remains a name for something that is out of balance, the origins of which are as obscure as those of the divine spark within us. The modern-day magician Dion Fortune wrote: "Evil is simply that which is moving in the opposite direction to evolution. [It] is that which . . . tends to revert to the unmanifest. Evil can be viewed . . . as the principle of inertia, which binds 'the good.' Good can be seen as the principle of creative movement, which resists inertia. We may be reminded of the terms 'Negative' and 'Positive' as a means of grasping these principles in a more helpful and less relative way. The way of Chaos, as an expression of the Negative pole, can be cleansing and effective, just as the way of creativity, as an expression of the Positive pole, can represent an imbalance of fertility. Which of these can be said to be good or evil?"

So what does the wizard offer as a contribution to the balanced way of evolution? Those who follow the way of the wizard are not the elect, they do not offer a dogmatic package to salvation; they are coworkers, mediators between micro- and macrocosm who believe in their tradition as a means of spiritual progression. This essential work is not the sole province of esotericists and magicians but belongs to all religious traditions, crafts, and skills. The mystic, poet, and artist—indeed, anyone who has an awareness that there is more to the world than what we perceive with our five senses—contribute to this work. If we look at the lives of several famous—or, rather, infamous—wizards, we will catch a glimpse of what made them seem evil to those who encountered them, as well as the way in which they were often misrepresented for other reasons.

# THE WIZARD OF EILDON

The path walked by the wizard can be both difficult and dangerous, balanced between the heights of heaven and the depths of hell. Dante placed many of the most famous wizards in the ninth circle of hell and described them as having their heads turned around so that they can see only backward. Among these unfortunate people is a wizard who was very clearly portrayed as having a foot in both camps. This is the medieval Scottish wizard Michael Scot, a perfect example of the kind of blurring of the moral edges that takes place around certain wizards. On the one hand, he is seen to have attended the "black" school in which he learned many of the darker arts. However, something always prevented him from crossing the line into the realm of black magic, and eventually he escaped with his life and soul intact. On other occasions, he was said to have crossed swords with the devil and to have forced the Prince of Darkness to serve him. For example, he once forced Lucifer to take the form of a horse and carry him from Scotland to France. Many stories tell of his work in designing and building houses for the Scottish gentry, who did not suspect that he was assisted by demons in much the same way that King Solomon received help in building the Temple in Jerusalem. On other occasions, Scot tricked the devil into splitting the Eildon Hills, a place with which Scot was ever after associated, into three—as they are to this day. He is thus seen as walking the narrow line between dark sorcery and white magic. This was a perilous place to be because he was relying on the forces of evil for his power while, at the same time, using that power only for good. Not all wizards succeed in this, but Scot seems to have done so.

This character is largely the product of folklore. The real Michael Scot (1175–1234) is known to have been the court astrologer to the Holy Roman emperor, Frederic II, himself accused of practicing dark magic. Born in Fife, Scotland, Scot traveled throughout Europe and was educated at the universities of Oxford, Paris, and Toledo. While in Spain he studied magic and the healing arts with the Arabs and discovered the remains of the Greek classical literature preserved there. His translations of Aristotle, as well as certain Arabic books on astrology, earned him a reputation as a scholar but darkened his name among those who feared and questioned the works of ancient writers. Nevertheless, his importance as a transmitter of arcane knowledge is beyond doubt, and his influence is seen in the writings of Bacon and Dee. His famous (or infamous) book of magic may not have been written by him at all, even though it bears his name. It may still be seen in the John Rylands Library in Manchester, England.

There are both Scottish and Italian traditions concerning Scot. One story is told of his death that perfectly illustrates his tricksterish nature and the fine line he walked between darkness and light. When he was near death, Scot sent a trusted man to hell to find out what was in store for him. The man returned with details of a particularly unpleasant bed of fire that had been set aside for Scot. When he heard this, the magician recanted his beliefs and died a reformed man. After his death his body was laid out on a mountainside and three ravens swooped toward it—a certain sign that Scot's soul was destined for the nether realm. However, before the dark birds could reach him, three white doves appeared and flew around his body. This was taken as a sign that Scot's soul was saved, just as a similar event was seen to indicate the redemption of the Brahan Seer.

According to an Italian account, Scot predicted that a small rock would fall on his head and kill him. In order to avoid this, he wore a metal cap beneath his hood. One day, however, he removed the cap when entering a church. At that precise moment a small stone fell and hit him on the head. Examining it, Scot declared that it was exactly the weight of the stone he had predicted would kill him. He put his affairs in order and died soon after, apparently as a result of the wound.

✦  ✦  ✦  ✦

Wherever we look, we find that those wizards who challenge the natural order of things or who make hugely vaunting claims are at best exaggerating and at worst falsifying their abilities. If we pause to look at the careers of two notorious "black" magicians we will find that surface accounts are not always what they seem.

**Book of Magic**
A page from the magic grimoire of Michael Scot.

# The Challenge of Simon Magus

One of the great classical wizards whose reputation has generally been associated with evil is Simon the Magician, better known as Simon Magus. Simon has become the epitome of the failed magician. His famous contest with St. Peter, in which he offered to take to the air like a bird to prove that Christianity was a false religion, ended in a plunge to the unyielding earth. Yet during his life Simon attracted a large following and showed himself by no means lacking in wisdom.

Having learned magic in Egypt, he became the leader of a Gnostic cult after a spectacular magical battle with its former head. His followers elevated him to the status of godhead; yet when his miracles were bettered by those of the disciple Philip, he renounced his former beliefs for a time and was baptized a Christian. Later, however, he reneged on his conversion, when he unsuccessfully tried to purchase the power of the Holy Spirit with money (an act from which we derive the modern term *simony*). After this, Simon became a deadly enemy of all Christians, contesting the miracles of the disciples at every turn until his fatal contest with Peter.

**Simon Magus**

A fifteenth-century painting of the conflict between St. Peter and the pagan wizard Simon Magus. The Emperor Nero watches from his throne.

There is, indeed, something almost tragic about Simon. He was immensely proud, as were many other wizards and magicians, and gave place to no man as an equal. This forced him to extend himself above any natural talents he might have possessed, and his fall was all the more spectacular because it followed claims that would have placed him far above any other similar figure of this time. He was pursued by signs that began increasingly to point to his disfavor. His own dog is said to have spoken out damningly, while a seven-month-old child apparently

**Simon Magus**
Despite demonic help, the wizard Simon Magus falls to his death in this thirteenth-century painting.

became a mouthpiece for heavenly accusations. Fearful now, Simon threw his magical books into the sea so that his enemies could never find them (and perhaps expose him as the charlatan he is widely believed to have been) and fled to Rome, where he still had a considerable following.

It was here that the last dramatic acts in Simon's life took place. The disciples Peter and Paul arrived in Rome, and the Emperor Nero summoned them, together with Simon, to publicly prove who was the strongest. Peter proposed a simple test—that Simon should read his mind. Nero's reaction was to place Simon in an even deeper hole by declaring that Simon must know these things since he was known to have raised the dead. To which Peter replied that he had not yet seen this miraculous power demonstrated.

Growing angry, now Simon threatened to call angels to his defense and cried out:

*"Let great dogs come forth and eat him [Peter] up before Caesar." And suddenly there appeared great dogs, and rushed at Peter. But Peter, stretching forth his hands to pray, showed to the dogs the loaf which he had blessed; which the dogs seeing, [they] no longer appeared. Then Peter said to Nero: "Behold, I have shown thee that I knew what Simon was thinking of, not by words but by deeds; for he, having promised that he would bring angels against me, has brought dogs, in order that he might show that he had not god-like but dog-like angels."*

*APOCRYPHAL ACTS OF THE HOLY APOSTLES PETER AND PAUL*

Backed into a corner by this, Simon played his last card, declaring that he would fly up to heaven the next day and challenging Peter to do the same. Nero, his curiosity now fully aroused, ordered a wooden tower to be erected in the Campus Martius and commanded that both ordinary people and senators should be present. The *Apocryphal Acts of the Holy Apostles Peter and Paul* gives a vivid account of what happened next:

*Then Simon went up upon the tower in the face of all, and crowned with laurels, he stretched forth his hands, and began to fly. And when Nero saw him flying, he said to Peter: "This Simon is true; but thou and Paul are deceivers." To whom Peter said: "Immediately shalt thou know that we are true disciples of Christ [while he is] but a magician, and a malefactor." Nero said: "Do you still persist? Behold, you see him going up to heaven. . . ." And Peter, looking steadfastly against Simon, said: "I adjure you, ye angels of Satan, who are carrying him into the air, to deceive the hearts of the unbelievers. . . . no longer to keep him up, but to let him go." And immediately, being let go, he fell into a place called Sacra Via. . . . and was broken into four parts.*

Peter's visionary gifts showed Nero the truth—that Simon was carried by invisible demons, who gave way before him and allowed the false magician to fall to the earth. Not surprisingly, this became a frequently repeated story of the victory of Christ's followers over those who chose to become the servants of evil.

But does this add to our understanding of the wizard? Certainly, it points to a way of interpreting the facts that is worth bearing in mind. Simon Magus has come down to us as, at best, a victim of spiritual pride and, at worst, a monster of depravity and a servant of evil—and the figure of the wizard has taken color from this ever since. Yet he later became the focus of a stream of Gnostic wisdom, and various sacred texts were attributed to him. Some of these became the seeds of a philosophical vision that still informs the work of the magician—suggesting the importance of looking not only at the surface facts but also at the political or religious reasons for the darkening of characters like Simon.

# †he Dark Monster

The myth of the black magician is a tale that has grown in the telling. Mostly it was the product of fear—fear of the Church's powerful arm of Inquisition, of the unknown, and of those who possessed powers not easily quantifiable. One of the best examples of this is Gilles de Rais (1404–1440). He is better known as Bluebeard, whose name has become almost synonymous with depravity, but who was once renowned as a courageous soldier and a marshal of France.

It was probably his association with Joan of Arc that turned people against Gilles initially, just as they turned against Joan herself when her extraordinary crusade failed and she was tried for heresy and condemned to death by fire. During her rise to power, Gilles had supported her, and it is likely that the accusations aimed at Joan, that she was a practitioner of black magic and in league with the devil, rubbed off onto Gilles. Before this, Gilles had been acknowledged as a noble and truehearted man, whose bravery on the field of battle was second to none. After the execution of Joan, he went into retirement, and it is at this juncture that stories began to circulate that pointed toward his own end. At first, he was accused of nothing more than extravagance, of living so well and in such luxury that it was not surprising if people wondered how he found the wherewithal to pay for it all. In fact, he was simply a very wealthy man, having inherited a vast fortune. But jealous acquaintances and ill-educated peasants suspected that Gilles's wealth was derived from a more sinister source. This belief led to more fantastic tales of his debauchery, sadism, and practice of dark magic.

Whether or not there was ever any truth to these accusations remains uncertain. When Gilles was finally summoned to appear before a conclave of judges, he began giving evidence boastfully and without care. However, more and more people came forward to bear witness to his dreadful acts, many from among his own household. He then became "increasingly fearful." Finally, under threat of torture, he confessed to so many unspeakable acts of murder, sodomy, and pedophilia that the chief judge was forced to place a cloth over the crucifix in the room where the court convened—as though the dreadful confessions should not be seen or witnessed by God.

The confession itself, which can still be read by those with a strong enough stomach, should probably not be given too much credence. Such outbursts, produced under threat of torture, seldom have roots in reality. Gilles may not even be the author of the document; such "confessions" were often written in advance and signed later by the unfortunate victim. What is interesting is the way that the confession draws on some profound and fundamental fears associated with wizards. They include the existence of demons and the practice of the black arts, ritual murder and infanticide, and human and demonic couplings. In reality, Gilles was probably not even a wizard at all. It was only after his death that the story of Bluebeard by Perrault made Gilles even more of a monster by describing the systematic murder of his wives. From here on, the legend grew, with ever more horrific acts attributed to Gilles. He was now seen to have confided in magicians and alchemists, both presented as practicing the black arts, and to have offered up countless child sacrifices to the devil in order to gain more wealth and to satisfy his unnatural lusts.

The truth of any of this may never be known, but the story of Gilles de Rais remains one of the darkest chapters in the history of the wizard. It shows just how easy it was for the superstitious and pious to perceive those who dared to overstep the limitations set by the Church in their quest for knowledge as perverse, twisted, and plainly evil.

That there existed a whole other genus of wizard better described as charlatans than as misunderstood thinkers who were ahead of their time is proved when we turn to the lives and adventures of two more famous wizards, Faust and Gerbert of Aurillac.

**Gilles de Rais**

Gilles de Rais, better known as "Bluebeard," was tried for numerous crimes in the fifteenth century. He was considered one of the most evil men ever to have lived.

# The Dreadful Bargain

**Faust**

A painting by Jose Garcia
Ramos (1875–1910)
depicting a scene from
Gounod's opera *Faust*.

Faust may well be considered another of those archetypal characters who, like Merlin and Prospero, have become synonymous with the figure of the wizard. Yet, in fact, the historical Faust was probably no more than a trickster and charlatan. He was made a legend in his own lifetime by his boastful claims to have hosts of demons at his beck and call; to be able to transmit the whole texts of various lost works by Aristotle, Terence, and Plautus; and to provide food and drink brought from far-off places in the blink of an eye.

Faust was certainly well educated, though his origins were probably humble. He is on record as having given lectures on Homer and the Roman poets, and his knowledge of early esoteric literature stood him in good stead in helping to substantiate his claims to be the foremost magician and sorcerer in Europe. However, if we examine his life closely and read the literature that has gathered around him, there is little or nothing to uphold his claims. What emerges is the picture of a rather pathetic figure who sought fame and fortune by claiming to be dangerous, wicked, and an unrepenting servant of the devil.

The actual dates of Faust's birth and death are vague. He was born sometime around the end of the fifteenth century in Germany, and the last references to his being alive date from 1540. After that the legends took over and produced the characters familiar to us today from Goethe's great poem and Christopher Marlowe's sensational play *Dr. Faustus*. Between these two points stretches a vast field of literary reference and storytelling. It is as though the story of Faust had its own life and kept growing, often out of all proportion to its origins.

A typical story dating from this period tells how Dr. Faust persuaded the University of Erfurt to let him give a series of lectures on Homer. These were immensely popular, and a number of students, who evidently knew of Faust's reputation as a necromancer, asked him to call up the shades of the characters from the *Iliad* and the *Odyssey*. Faust obliged by producing a whole spectrum of Greek heroes, from Achilles to Agamemnon. He finally ended on a high note by bringing forth the one-eyed giant Polyphemus, complete with a half-eaten corpse hanging from his mouth. After striking the floor a number of times with his great iron spear and threatening to eat several of the students, the giant vanished, leaving Faust's reputation several degrees higher than before. Of course he may well have engineered this feat simply by having actors stationed in the wings. Indeed, many of Faust's manifestations of his magical skills could be explained in a similar manner.

One of the best stories of this kind comes from a collection of Faustian myths called *The Erfurt Chronicle*. Dating from around 1580, this story was presumably

written within a few years of Faust's death. It comes shortly after another episode, in which some of Faust's friends, missing him and knowing him to be in Prague at the time, summoned him in their thoughts. He appeared immediately, riding a fiery horse, and provided them with several kinds of rare wine that he apparently produced from nowhere. Shortly after this he returned again from Prague, bearing gifts for his friends and inviting them to visit him for a grand feast. Let us take up the story from here.

# DR. FAUST COMES TO DINNER

The company arrived in his rooms at St. Michael's Inn, but there was no sign of any preparation for their stay. Faust came in and knocked on the table with a knife. Soon a servant entered and the following dialogue took place:

"Sir, what do you wish?"

Faust answered: "How quick are you?"

"As an arrow."

"Not quick enough. You shall not serve me. Go back to wherever you came from."

Again Faust knocked, and when another servant entered he asked the same question: "How quick are you?"

"As the wind," said he.

"That is something, but not enough," said Dr. Faust, and sent him out.

**Faust**

An early etching shows Dr. Faust summoning a demon from within the safety of a magic circle.

When he knocked a third time, another servant entered and when he was asked the same question, said he was quick as the thoughts of man.

"Good," said Dr. Faust, "you'll do." Then he went outside with the man and told him what he should do. He returned again to his guests and asked them to wash their hands and sit down. Soon the servant with two others brought in three covered dishes for each person at the table, and this happened four times. Thirty-six courses were served, with game, fowl, vegetables, meat-pies and other meat, not to mention fruit, confections, cakes, etc.

All the beakers, glasses, and mugs were put on the table empty. Then Dr. Faust asked each one what he wished to drink in the way of beer and wine. He then put the cups outside of the window and soon took them back again, every one of them full of the fresh drink that each one had requested.

The music that another of his servants played was so charming that his guests had never heard the like, and so wonderful as if several were playing in harmony on harmoniums, fifes, lutes, harps, trumpets, etc. So they made merry until broad daylight.

✦  ✦  ✦  ✦

**Faust**
Mephistopheles tempts Dr. Faust to all he can see, in an echo of Christ's temptation by the Devil.

Once again, there is nothing here that could not have been contrived by simple stage management, but it does give a glimpse into the kind of magical activity attributed to Faust at this point in time.

After *The Erfurt Chronicle*, works that retold the story of Faust multiplied—as did the wild and wonderful tales told about him. The *Faustbook* of 1587 added what is perhaps the most famous incident in the life of this particular wizard—his pact with the devil so memorably related by Goethe and Marlowe. In this early version, a Franciscan monk named Dr. Minge attempts to dissuade Faust from following the road to damnation and to recant his dealing with Lucifer.

This became the central matter in the Faust legend from here on, with his devilish pact and the events following it occupying a more and more important role in his story. In addition, he was now credited with calling up the spirit of the beautiful Helen of Troy in order to mate with her and produce a "spirit-child" named Justus, who vanished when his father died. Other feats attributed to Faust run the whole gamut of wizardly skills from several centuries and numerous other practitioners. He could, it was said, produce rain on demand; build palaces from thin air; and render people temporarily blind, dumb, or paralyzed.

Descriptions of Faust's last night on Earth are dramatic and often moving. It seems that the old wizard repented at the last and begged for forgiveness and the return of his soul. The devil mocked him for this, reviling him in terms that had more to do with the current Lutheran hatred for Catholic mysticism than with the evils of a simple magician. The students, who seem to have always loved Faust, joined in his prayers, but in vain. In the night terrible cries were heard to come from his chamber, and in the morning his body was found ripped into hundreds of pieces.

Faust's rise and fall reflect the times in which he lived. Superstitious fears of the unknown, as well as belief in evil and darkness, lay as close to hand as goodness and light. Together with the religious struggles of the time (it is no accident that Martin Luther himself mentions Faust as a figure of evil), accounts of these fears show us that the wizard was perceived through the sixteenth century and beyond as a servant of evil and a practitioner of dark and dangerous arts. The legacy of Faust—like that of Gilles de Rais, Michael Scot, and Gerbert de Aurillac—has colored the image of the wizard ever since. Few accounts of the wizard would be complete without his negative counterpart. Harry Potter must have his Voldemort; Gandalf his Saruman.

# The Wizard Pope

One of the most unlikely places to look for a so-called black magician is among the list of medieval popes. Yet several popes were believed to practice necromancy and to be in league with the devil. Historically, this reflects the disillusion with Rome that brought about the Reformation. But underlying the curious tales of prelates who practiced magic is the same theme that runs throughout this whole chapter—that of the possession of knowledge and power, and its misuse. The popes wielded absolute spiritual power over the Christian world and also had great political power. Small wonder then that we find no less than eighteen "black" popes, stretching in an unbroken line from John XII (965–972) to Gregory VII (1073–1085).

In 1479, Bartholomew Platina, an assistant librarian at the Vatican, published his *Opus in Vitas Summorum Pontificum*, in which he outlined the many sinister and satanic dealings between the popes and the devil. Among those whose lives come under scrutiny is Sylvester II, who wore the papal crown from 999 to 1003. His real name was Gerbert de Aurillac, and we can be fairly certain that he did indeed practice magic, besides fulfilling the role of the wizard in a number of other ways.

Gerbert was born at Aurillac in France toward the end of the tenth century. An unusually gifted man, he appears to have studied in Moorish Spain, either at Toledo or Cordoba, where he learned alchemy and the traditional heritage of Western magic. A colorful story relates the means by which he came by his magical powers. Lodging in the house of a wise and wealthy Moor, Gerbert soon discovered that his host possessed an ancient magical grimoire (a printed collection of rituals and spells) of great power. Gerbert resolved to obtain this treasure, but the Arabian philosopher refused flatly to part with it or to reveal where it was hidden. Gerbert found out from his host's daughter, whom he seduced, that the old man kept it hidden under his pillow at night. After this it was a simple matter to get his host drunk, steal the book, and escape with it. However, because the old Moor was skilled in astrology, he could determine Gerbert's location as long as he was on either earth or water. The fugitive tricked him by hanging upside down under a bridge so that he touched neither element. He then fled to the shore of the sea and used the book to call up the devil, who flew him back across the sea to his home.

From here on, Gerbert's rise to power was rapid. Having set his heart on the papacy, he signed away his soul and was soon elevated to the Chair of Peter. Taking the name Sylvester II, Gerbert began a life of debauchery and intrigue by using his office to obtain riches and women. At the same time he began to consider how long he might live to enjoy these delights before the day came when his soul would be claimed. The answer was reassuring: As long as he failed to celebrate mass in Jerusalem his reign would continue. Thus content with his lot, the magician-pope set about enjoying a thoroughly hedonistic and luxurious life. Then one day as he was dispensing the sacraments in a small church near the edge of the city, he felt his strength begin to ebb. On learning that the name of the church was the Holy Cross of Jerusalem he knew that his moment had come. Crying out that he was surrounded by demons, he fell to the earth and confessed everything.

With his last breath, Gerbert gave instructions that his body should be cut into pieces and his coffin placed on a bier of green wood drawn by two horses, one white and the other black. They were to be left to go where they would and his remains interred where they stopped. All was done as Gerbert had requested. The strange cortege wound its way through the streets of Rome until it came to the Lateran church, where the horses stopped. This was seen as a sign that Sylvester had been reprieved, and he was duly interred in the church. Afterward it was said that cries and moans issued from the coffin for several hours before a deathly silence fell. His tomb later shook or wept tears whenever a pope was about to die.

The truth about Gerbert is that he was no more than a highly intelligent man who was possessed of real vision. Tradition says that he was the first person to introduce Arabic numerals to the West and that he brought the earliest clocks into the Vatican. From this, it was but a short step to believing that he had invented them. So, as were many other wizards of the time, he was known as an inventor as well as a magician. As in so many of the examples explored here, the possession of wisdom and knowledge of a perfectly ordinary kind was often easily perceived as more arcane and sinister. For a time Gerbert occupied the most powerful position in the Western world. His spectacular fall from grace and his confession of demonic aid rocked the Christian world, adding fuel to the ferment that would eventually bring about the Reformation.

**Sylvester II**

According to some accounts, Pope Sylvester II (999–1003) confessed to being a practitioner of magic when he felt death approaching him.

# An Eminent Trickster

nother facet of the wizard is that of the trickster. Ancient tales from
locations as diverse as Egypt and North America present images of
archetypal figures who were semidivine. They taught by way of tricks
and tests that were generally practiced on poor foolish humans. In
medieval times Merlin was not averse to behaving in this manner. Later such
characters as Puck appeared whose magic was definitely of a tricksterish kind.

  At a more simple, human level, there are those who have plied the wizard's
trade and made the best for themselves, building vast reputations on subtle
observance and psychological manipulation. One of the most famous of these
trickster magicians was the eighteenth-century count Alexander Cagliostro
(1743–1795), who by dint of superior intellect baffled most of the crowned heads
of Europe for more than thirty years.

As you might expect from a character of this kind, Cagliostro's exact origins are debated. Some say his real name was Guiseppi Balsom, born in Palermo to a poor Sicilian family. Others tell the story of a poor but street-savvy child who learned to make good use of his natural psychic gifts and soon escaped from poverty to fame and fortune. When he was twenty-three he traveled to the island of Malta and there joined the Order of the Knights of Malta and studied such arcane subjects as kabbala, alchemy, and magic. Some time after this he is said to have borrowed the name Cagliostro from his godmother and traveled to England, where he joined the Freemasons.

For most of his life thereafter he roamed the royal courts of Europe, England, and Russia. In Italy he met and married Lorenza Feliciani, who joined him in various esoteric business opportunities, including fortune-telling, scrying (fortune-telling done by looking into a mirror or other polished object), crystal gazing, and the selling of magical potions. Several times they claimed to have discovered the elixir of life or the philosopher's stone, or both, and made money from selling them to gullible individuals. They held seances, called up and banished demons, and practiced hypnotism.

For a time, Cagliostro could do no wrong. Then, in 1875, both he and Lorenza were implicated in a scandalous plot to swindle Queen Marie Antoinette out of 1.6 million francs for the creation of a diamond necklace that was subsequently stolen. The Cagliostros escaped punishment by telling a fantastic story of the so-called count's birth and upbringing in Arabia and his vast fortune, which made it nonsense to suspect him of involvement in a petty crime. Fleeing to England, Cagliostro predicted the forthcoming French Revolution—though it could be said that he would have not required any great occult skills to do this. Shortly after, a London newspaper published an exposé of the true birth and life of the famous count, and once again the pair fled—this time to Rome, where a few months later they were both arrested and accused of heresy, witchcraft, and the practice of black magic. Found guilty, Cagliostro was sentenced to death, while Lorenza was to suffer life imprisonment in a convent. In the end, however, the pope commuted the count's sentence to life and he was confined in an underground cell in the San Leo prison. There, according to whichever story you believe, he either died or miraculously escaped four years later. Lorenza, however, perished in the convent.

During his lifetime, Cagliostro probably did much to keep alive the idea of the occult practitioner and was frequently referred to as "the divine wizard." His dramatic fall from grace, and the numerous exposés published after his demise, made many people more cautious about what they believed.

**Occult practice**
A wizard scrying the future from a bowl of water, as depicted in an early book on magic.

# The Holy Devil

No examination of the darker side of magic and its practitioners would be complete without a brief look at the remarkable figure of Grigory Rasputin (1871–1916), a figure so cloaked in mystery that even today, almost one hundred years after his spectacular demise, no one has successfully explained some of the feats of magic that he apparently achieved. Yet Rasputin's life and acts are colored not by religious fervor so much as by political expediency. His life is inextricably wound around the events leading up to the Russian Revolution and the fall of the czars, and it is these events that have colored accounts of this strange, larger-than-life figure.

Rasputin, whose name means literally "the dissolute," belonged to a sect known as the Khlysty, or Flagellants, whose central doctrine was salvation through sin. It practiced a form of ancient magic that devolved, ultimately, from the orgiastic rites of ancient Greece. Ecstasy was evoked through scourging, alcohol, debauchery, and drugs. This bizarre way of life cruelly mixed love and lust to a degree where one resembled another. Rasputin himself displayed aspects of the fiend and the saint, the depraved and the divinely inspired. Childlike in one breath and demonic in the next, he was appropriately named the Holy Devil. But it was the power he exerted over czar Nicholas II and the czarina Alexandra that lifted Rasputin from the everyday world of superstition and placed him at center stage of that era of political unrest and revolution. Some commentators have attributed the spark that set fire to the Russian people to Rasputin, declaring that his demonic magic was responsible for turning the czar's few supporters against him and provoking the first acts of revolt.

Rasputin's early years were eventful enough. He was born in Pokrovskoye to Siberian peasants who were themselves descendants of the shamans of the Altai region. Working as a carter, he earned a reputation as a womanizer with a prodigious appetite

**Rasputin**
The mystic Grigory Rasputin was feared for his magical powers and his influence over the last czar and czarina of Russia.

for drink. Married at twenty, he then took to farming, until the death of his son in infancy drove him to undertake a pilgrimage to Mt. Athos in Greece. There he apparently experienced a vision of the Virgin Mary, and when he returned home he declared himself a *starets*, a kind of freelance mystic.

Moving to St. Petersburg, Rasputin quickly became a popular figure who was equally loved and hated, feared and admired. Drawn into the circles of the nobility, he came to the attention of the royal family when word of his formidable healing skills became widely known. The only male heir to the throne of Russia, Alexis, suffered from hemophilia, the inability of his blood to clot. Rasputin proved to be the only person able to heal the boy whenever he became ill. But the increasing power exercised by the Holy Devil over the Romanoffs—especially Alexandra, who adored him—made Rasputin an object of greater and greater jealousy among the ruling nobility. Finally, a plot was set in motion to kill him.

In a letter written in 1915, Rasputin predicted that he would be killed before January 1 of the following year. He added that if it was a peasant who killed him the monarchy would continue to prosper, but that if a member of the aristocracy did the deed then the royal family would perish within twenty-five years.

**Rasputin**
Alan Rickman portraying
Rasputin in the 1996 *Grigory
Rasputin* television production.

Both of his predictions proved to be true. Rasputin was indeed murdered, under circumstances that can only be called bizarre, on the night of December 29, 1916. An account of the events of that night by Prince Felix Yusupov, one of the perpetrators in the plot to kill Rasputin, is well worth recounting, if only for its innate drama.

Yusupov and his three accomplices had invited Rasputin to dine with them and had liberally laced his drink with poison. What followed was horrific and testified as much to the awe exerted by Rasputin over his murderers as to his innate power as a magician.

The killers waited in vain for the poison to take effect as Rasputin continued to talk and to demand yet more to drink. Finally, two hours later, Yusupov shot him at point-blank through the heart and saw him fall, apparently dead, on the floor of the dining room.

Later, as the conspirators sat together, drinking and congratulating each other on the success of their plot, Yusupov was seized by a vague feeling of alarm. He returned to the dining room and bent over the body of Rasputin. As he did so the magician sat up and tried to grip the prince by the throat.

Terrified, Yusupov shot his victim again, three times, and beat him about the head with an iron bar. Then, together with his conspirators, he dragged the body of the magician outside, bound his arms and legs, and flung him through a hole into the frozen river Neva. When the police discovered the body forty-eight hours later, the ropes that had bound him had been broken and there were no traces of either gunshot wounds or poison. The cause of death was declared to be drowning, and it was said that the ice betrayed signs of the scratching of desperate fingers as Rasputin strove to get free.

Much of this account doubtless owes its origins to older stories of Siberian wizards believed to be virtually immortal, while the fear generated by Rasputin seems to have affected everyone. Attempts to obscure the murderous nature of the events may also have contributed. But there is little doubt that Rasputin's death demonstrated a belief in his astonishing powers, regardless of whether or not he actually possessed them.

His predictions regarding the fate of Russia were proved true. The Russian royal family were murdered two years later, and the resulting upheaval, followed by the onset of World War I, brought the monarchy to the brink of extinction. The last flickering flame of the aristocracy was finally doused exactly twenty-five years after Rasputin's death, with the coming to power of Stalin and the dawn of World War II.

The truth about Rasputin is that he was more of a shaman than a monk or a magician, and that the brand of magic he practiced, labeled demonic, was more of a throwback to the ancient folk religion of Russia. Yet the Holy Devil possessed many of the attributes we have come to recognize as belonging to the wizard: He was a healer, a visionary prophet, and virtually impossible to kill. He may not have carried a staff or crystal ball, consulted magic books, or (at least openly) uttered spells or curses. Yet for all that, he strikes us as a misunderstood figure whose strange mixture of saint and sinner was too large and powerful for his contemporaries to deal with. That, together with his influence over the czar and czarina, doomed him not only to be killed but also to have a reputation that was forever blackened in the eyes of the world. However, he seems never to have actually done bodily harm to anyone, and his advice and prophetic insights were proved true time and again. In many respects Rasputin was a man out of time, a wizard wandering at the dawn of the twentieth century, when political power was reckoned more important than any brand of magic, in a land that was torn asunder between a belief in ancient religious roots and the emerging power of Communism.

**Rasputin**

Rasputin photographed with courtiers of czar Nicholas II, late 1800s.

# EMPEROR OF THE DARK

Modern images of the "evil" wizard tend to point to the excesses and boastful claims of men like Rasputin. This is not the place to weigh the truth or otherwise of such people, though their stories do demonstrate that the myth of the black magician is far from dead. Contemporary examples of this are to be found in a hundred practitioners of dark magic who fill the pages of recent fantasy literature—much of it highly colored and sensational.

In the modern myth *Star Wars*, which has captured so much of the continuing history of magic and wizardry, the evil magician is represented by the emperor Palpatine. He is a representative of the dark lords of the Sith, a breakaway sect from those who follow the way of the mystical Force that animates the universe. George Lucas, who has acknowledged the influence of the great modern mythographer Joseph Campbell, draws many themes from ancient myths to create his world of battling heroes and heroines, including the popularized concept of the light and dark magicians. In the *Star Wars* epic, the Jedi knight, Obi-Wan Kenobi, is a type of the gifted wizard working for the light side of the Force, while Palpatine stands for generations of dark practitioners.

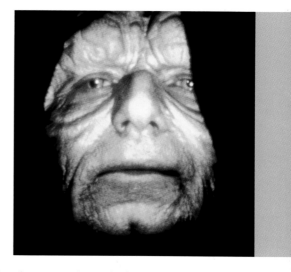

**Star Wars**
The emperor Palpatine (played by Ian McDiarmid) in George Lucas's epic film series *Star Wars* represents a figure of infinite evil.

A whole complex of material has built up around this figure. Additional information from the numerous novels, comic books, and games set in the *Star Wars* universe round out the figure sketched so vividly in the movies. Thus, we hear of Palpatine's gradual rise to political power from humble origins as a senator of the planet of Naboo. He seems always to have been a member of the Sith, dark magicians who followed the polarized Dark Side of the Force.

He is attributed with compiling a collection of writings known as *The Book of Anger*, reminiscent of the books written by many of the famous wizards we have discussed. In common with many wizards through the ages, both light and dark, Palpatine is difficult to kill, passing in spirit form from body to body until finally bound to the soul of a Jedi master and thus carried into the sphere of the Light Side. His powers are every bit as awesome as those displayed by wizards of the older school, and in all he embodies many of the characteristics of those explored above. As with *The Lord of the Rings* and the Harry Potter books, the *Star Wars* series shows that the era of the wizard is far from dead and that the dark brotherhood continues to flourish alongside those who follow the light.

# DEFENSE AGAINST THE DARK

**W**izards are often shown casting circles of protection that will enable them to summon spirits to do their bidding without harm to themselves. There is much about this that is highly colored and even fictional. In reality, wizards seldom if ever summon spirits, and when they do so it is in full awareness that they are entering into an alliance with the being in question to enable an action to take place that is in alignment with the workings of the cosmos. To put it another way, responsible wizards will not undertake a magical act of any kind without the awareness that it is being carried out with the compliance of the universe or according to the law of God. Thus, when we speak of magical defense, we are entering into a realm full of thorny questions.

The first thing to be aware of is that the world is not full of people launching evil energies against you—to believe this is to invest in a kind of personal self-importance that suggests that you are actually important enough to warrant such an attack! The second thing to be aware of is that the best basic protection against anything negative of this kind is a basic human awareness of what feels right. Thus, it is best to refuse the offer of a person who wants to do a piece of magical work to help you win the heart of someone you love but who seems unattainable. Your instincts will tell you whether to trust the person making the offer, and it is wiser to listen to them!

hat said, there can be times when you find yourself open to negative energies. The ill will of an enemy can sometimes seem to take an almost tangible form, and this is rightly something to guard against. The world of the magician is by no means all black and white. A great deal has been written concerning black magic that is best left to the pages of sensational fiction. But it would be foolish to think that there were no negative forces in the world. The truth of the matter is somewhat more subtle and involves the recognition that there are fewer actual dark forces than there is simply power that is open to misuse as well as to anything else. A true definition of black magic is the use of power for the self to gain control over others. A white wizard knows better than this and would use such power that has been given (fully understanding that it can be taken away again) only for good, and only in line with the higher forces of the universe.

This requires a basic acceptance of the fact that there are laws governing the uses and misuses of magic. It is actually far harder to send out a curse or to attempt a spell to bind another person than it is to offer help or blessings. In the former instance, as we have seen, the wizard requires the cooperation of negative spirits that are usually bound to his will. Not only is such an action not undertaken lightly, it does not come without a price. In the second instance, help is always available and willingly given without strings attached.

Much of this has to do with the individual intention. Even good intentions can be fraught with dangers to the ego and to the free will of the other person. Always ask the permission of the person you desire to work for. Never go in with good intentions but without an understanding of the whole situation.

Certain practices have been understood over the ages as basic acts of protection suitable for any magical practitioner. The most basic and familiar is the circle. If created with intent, the circle does not even need to be drawn on the earth in the traditional manner. The simple imagining of a circle of protection is often sufficient, and the circle becomes more impenetrable with practice. However, if you decide that

**Inscribe a circle**
A modern wizard draws a protective circle on the ground.

the actual creation of such a circle is more in line with magical tradition, invoke the protection of your guardian angel or spirit and then inscribe the circle by drawing a line of light in the air around you. By standing within such a circle, you are protected against anything that you do not consciously invite in or take with you.

You might also wish to consider invoking your Holy Guardian Angel, a far more potent force than the simple guardian angel prescribed for us in childhood. This is a mighty being whose aid and protection, once invoked, is as effective as any circle or imaginary cloak of protection we might create. There are many invisible spirits in the universe, many of whom are willing to be our spiritual allies. In many cases the simple inward evoking of one of these is as effective as an elaborate ceremony. However, if you find yourself in need of help

(for example, if a sudden influx of fear challenges you), the following simple invocation will bring relief. Find a place where you will be undisturbed for a few minutes. Stand still and face the east, which is the direction of the rising sun and a good place from which to call for help. Close your eyes and imagine a circle of light drawn upon the floor around you.

Think of the problem that has arisen, or contemplate the fear that surrounds you. Call upon your Holy Guardian Angel, visualizing this mighty being in whatever form seems most appropriate to you, using the words on the opposite page or others which you have written.

Wait for a few moments until you feel the strength and presence of your Holy Guardian Angel. Allow it to permeate you, heart and soul, and then go forth secure in the knowledge that you are protected.

*Holy and Blessed Guardian Angel,*
*I call upon you to surround me with your light,*
*To protect me with your love,*
*To strengthen me in all that I do,*
*To go before me and to follow in my steps,*
*To protect me on my left and on my right,*
*Until the fear has passed,*
*Until the danger is gone,*
*Until I find my rest.*

**The Alchemist**
An alchemist in his laboratory
searches for the philosopher's
stone in this painting by Joseph
Wright of Derby (1795).

5 | The Wizard as Alchemist and Creator

# Technicians of the Sacred

All hail to the noble company
Of true students in holy alchemy,
Whose noble practice does them teach
To veil their secrets within misty speech.

ELIAS ASHMOLE, *THEATRUM CHEMICUM BRITANNICUM*

## The Stone of the Philosophers

We have now seen the wizard in several guises—as seer, as manipulator of the elements, and, above all, as someone who walked a fine line between saint and sinner. There is a part of the wizard's history that brings together a number of these aspects and adds a further dimension. The search for the stone of the philosophers can be seen as a search for eternal life and for a way to transform the riches of lead into gold. This was the work of the alchemists—the wizards of the Renaissance.

The philosopher's stone is a main focus of the first of the Harry Potter books. We never learn much about this stone other than that it is a talisman of great power. However, it is clear that wizards have been seeking it for a very long time. The stone has been accredited with many qualities, from the gift of giving life to the ability to change base metal into gold. It is central to the practice of protoscience and the work of the alchemists.

Alchemy itself has a long and complex history. It is said to have originated in ancient Egypt or even in Atlantis. It continued to flourish, particularly from the Middle Ages through the Renaissance. With the dawn of the so-called Age of

Enlightenment in the eighteenth century, it gradually gave way to science. Alchemy is primarily concerned with what we might call the science of magic, an investigation into the very structure of the cosmos.

The best-known kind of alchemy concentrates on making gold or discovering the elixir of life. But there was a spiritual alchemy also, and this is in many ways closer to the real magic of the wizard. The goal of this kind of alchemy is to refine the baser qualities of the human soul and turn them into the gold of spiritual enlightenment. Nicholas Flamel is credited in the Harry Potter story as having succeeded in the creation of the philosopher's stone. In the middle of the fourteenth century Flamel wrote:

> Our work is the conversion and change of one being into another being, as from one thing into another thing, from debility to strength . . . from corporeality to spirituality.

The effects of the stone are always described in terms of transformation. Its powers include sustaining life far beyond a normal span, healing illnesses, and possibly even defeating death itself. A significant account of the stone and its properties is found in a medieval text that deals with the quest for another wondrous object—the Holy Grail. German poet Wolfram von Eschenbach, writing around 1210, attributed the original source for his poem *Parzival* to one Kyot of Provence. He, in turn, had learned the secrets of the Grail from a Jewish astrologer named Flegitanis who lived in Toledo. Now Toledo, as we have seen, was a center for occult learning. Such wizards as Michael Scot studied there, believing it a perfect place to search for the sects of the philosopher's stone.

Flegitanis is also reputed to have known the lore of the stars, including a certain stone called the Grail that had been left on the Earth by angels. This is followed by a description that leaves us in no doubt at all of its identity. It seems that a body of knights, dedicated to the protection of the mysterious object, live in the great castle of Muntsalvach:

> They live from a stone of the purest kind. If you do not know it, it shall here be named to you. It is called lapsit exillis. By the power of that stone the phoenix burns to ashes, but the ashes give him life again. Thus does the phoenix molt and change its plumage, which afterwards is bright and shining and as lovely as before. There never was a human so ill but that, if he one day sees that stone, he cannot die within the week that follows. And in looks he will not fade. His appearance will stay the same, be it maid or man, as on the day he saw the stone, the same as when the best years of his life began, and though he should see the stone for two hundred years, it will never change, save that his hair might perhaps turn grey. Such power does the stone give a man that flesh and bones are at once made young again. The stone is also called the Grail.    (Parzival)

The Latin phrase *lapsit exillis* is almost certainly a corruption of *lapis ex caelis*, or "stone from heaven," suggesting that the stone was not originally of this Earth. It may well have been a meteorite like the black stone that lies within the Muslim Kaaba, a rectangular structure regarded as the center of the Muslim world, but its effects are exactly the same as the philosopher's stone: It preserves life and causes the kind of physical restitution that the phoenix experiences.

This, then, was a central goal of alchemist-wizards through the ages: to discover or create the stone that would offer eternal life and health along with the great power and wealth that would inevitably result. The list of those who sought it is long and contains some surprising names.

Nicholas Flamel, John Dee, Roger Bacon, and the emperor Rudolf II all spent much of their lives in search of the fabled stone. In addition, both the great scientist Isaac Newton and the distinguished psychoanalyst Carl Jung joined this important quest. Jung's studies produced concepts that coincide with those of alchemy.

**The Holy Grail**
Galahad, Perceval, and Bors receive a vision of the Holy Grail in this painting by Dante Gabriel Rossetti.

# Seekers of the Stone

We know Isaac Newton best today as a scientist and mathematician, but what is less well known is his lifelong fascination with alchemy and magic. For many, this great man represents what the visionary poet William Blake called "Single vision and Newton's sleep," a kind of mechanistic, blinkered approach to the universe that can be seen as the very definition of science. So it may seem ironic that he should also have been fascinated by magic. During the twenty-seven years that Newton was at Cambridge University he wrote *The Mathematical Principles of Natural Philosophy*, a book that revolutionized the work of the scientific community. However, he also spent these years intensely studying occult lore and magic. As the economist John Maynard Keynes wrote after examining the contents of a box containing many of Newton's most alchemical works:

> *Newton was not the first of the age of reason. He was the last of the age of the magicians . . . the last great mind that looked out on the visible and intellectual world with the same eyes as those which began to build our intellectual inheritance rather less than 10,000 years ago. . . . He was the last wonder-child to whom the Magi could do sincere and appropriate homage.*

This places Newton squarely in the ranks of the latter-day magicians.

Jung, the founder of depth psychology, may also strike us as an unlikely character to place among the ranks of the wizards—until, that is, we read some words he wrote almost at the end of his life:

> *Only after I had familiarized myself with alchemy did I realize that the unconscious is a process, and that the psyche is transformed or developed by the relationship of the ego to the contents of the unconscious. . . . Through the study of these collective transformation processes and through an understanding of alchemical symbolism I arrived at the central concept of my psychology: the process of individuation.*
>
> C. J. JUNG, *MEMORIES, DREAMS, REFLECTIONS*

This is exactly the concept of spiritual alchemy, which seeks to transform the soul and spirit of the individual into the gold of enlightenment. In fact, this transformation can be brought about only through the powers of the philosopher's stone.

*Top* **Isaac Newton**
The famous mathematician Isaac Newton had a lifelong interest in alchemy and magic.

*Above* **Carl Jung**
The psychologist Carl Jung sought for much of his life to fathom the truth of alchemical symbolism.

# Magic Stones

The philosopher's stone is only one of a number of magical stones that became part of the wizard's arsenal of power. In New Zealand, Maori wizards are called *tohungas*. They are figures who hark back to the shamanic practitioners of pre-Stone Age times, and even to the Celtic druids, with whom they share several characteristics such as the wearing of feathered cloaks; but they also possess certain of the traditional wizard's qualities and status. All are great, respected figures who combine the function of priest with that of magician. A description by a nineteenth-century missionary might well apply to any of the wizards we have been examining:

> *An old man apparently about eighty years of age, with a long flowing beard, white as snow, appearing as mysterious and singular in all his movements and converse as you might expect such a person to be . . . [his son] told me his father was the oldest man in the country . . . he had been proof against all disease; and, though he had accompanied the tribe on many a war expedition, no spear could pierce him, and no gun had power to pierce his sacred breast.*
>
> THOMAS BUDDLE, 1851

This immunity from disease and injury was attributed to a sacred red stone. The old tohunga's son told the same observer that he would swallow the stone when his father became too decrepit to continue. The son would thereby take upon himself all the old man's powers, and the father would be allowed to die peacefully. As in the case of Kenneth Odran, the Brahan Seer, it is the stone itself that not only provides visions but also contains the power of the wizard.

**Tohunga**
A Maori elder invokes the power of a tohunga's stone, said to contain the power of an individual wizard.

# Buildings Made of Air

The possession of a stone of power is connected with working with the elements. This, as we saw in Chapter 3, is a major aspect of the wizard's power. It leads in turn to the magical creation of artifacts—an extension of alchemy at its most scientific. Thus Merlin creates the Round Table for Arthur—round in imitation of the world—where all men may sit as equals. He is also famed for building Stonehenge, which he fetches from Ireland to make a fitting mausoleum for the dead king Aurelius. Geoffrey of Monmouth describes it vividly:

**The Round Table**

Merlin was credited with the construction of King Arthur's Round Table, where all sat as equals.

> *When they came to the stone structure . . . Merlin came up to them as they stood round in a group. "Try your strength, young men," said he. . . . At his bidding they all set to with every conceivable kind of mechanism . . . but none of these things advanced them an inch. When he saw what a mess they were making of it, Merlin burst out laughing. He placed in position all the gear he thought necessary and dismantled the stones more easily than you could ever believe . . . thus proving that his artistry was worth more than any brute strength.*
>
> (Trans. Lewis Thorpe)

Among Merlin's other skills are his ability to create the illusion of castles filled with food-laden tables, as well as dancers and musicians—all made from insubstantial air. Merlin also arranged for a wall of brass to circle the town of Carmarthen to keep out invaders and other evils. As Edmund Spenser records in *The Faerie Queene*:

> *Before that Merlin died, he did intend,*
> *A brazen wall in compass to compile*
> *About Cairmardin, and did it commend*
> *Unto these sprites, to bring to perfect end.*
> *. . . these fiends may not their work forbare,*
> *So greatly his commandmant they fear*
> *But there do toile and travel day and night*
> *Until that brazen wall they do uprear.*
>
> (CANTO III, VS. 10–11)

Like Solomon before him, Merlin commands spirits to do his work for him, drawing them from the Otherworld and instructing them to provide whatever he needs.

**Merlin and Stonehenge**

According to the twelfth-century writer Geoffrey of Monmouth, Merlin brought the stones for the building of Stonehenge from Ireland with the power of his magic.

# Artificers of Magic

erlin was not alone in the ranks of the wonder-working magicians who were able to create remarkable things. Virgil, who we remember was given something of a literary reincarnation as a medieval wizard, filled his home with strange devices powered by magic. Like the British wizard, he also created objects to protect his hometown, among them a bronze fly and a golden leech. Mechanical horsemen on mechanical steeds patroled the streets of Naples, while a brazen horse, made by magic, protected every beast of burden in the town from suffering from painful backs. The magical healing baths he built at Puteoli cured every disease known to humans. This allowed Virgil to demonstrate the power of his magic to heal in much the same way as the ancient shamans had done centuries earlier.

But perhaps Virgil's finest work was a huge device known as the *salvatio Romae*, designed to give advance warning of any attack on the Eternal City. Erected on Capitoline Hill, it rang a bell and pointed in the direction from which danger was likely to come. Carthaginians, however, infiltrated the city and, under the pretense of digging for hidden gold, undermined the foundations of the automaton so that it fell and broke. After Virgil's death all of his magical inventions were destroyed, but his reputation remains as the first creator of machines with the ability to "think" for themselves.

Both Virgil and Merlin could call upon spirits to carry out their great works of construction, but their skills pale when compared with King Solomon's achievements. According to *The Book of the Cave of Treasures*, King Solomon built the city of Palmyra in the midst of the wilderness, Heliopolis on the flanks of the mountain of the sun, and Arvad in the midst of the sea—all without human workers. Yet, as we saw in Chapter 1, his greatest feat was the building of the great Temple at Jerusalem. A magic ring gave him the power to summon devils and demons to undertake the design and building not only of the temple itself but also of several palaces and finally of his magnificent throne that was endowed with magical properties.

According to the Koran, the work on the temple was still incomplete when Solomon knew that his death was near at hand. Knowing that his death would leave his dream unfulfilled, he begged God to allow him to hide the fact from the jinn (spirits) who were laboring on the temple. His wish was granted, and when death claimed him he remained standing, propped up by his staff.

After a whole year had passed, a worm that had been gnawing on the staff finally ate through the wood, causing Solomon's body to fall to the ground. The spirits stopped work at once, after which arguments began as to whether the temple was actually completed or not.

All of these stories show us a different power of the wizard, using magic to become an artificer. From these comparatively simple exercises in harnessing the power of wind and water was the emergence of the ability to manipulate elements of creation itself to perform wonders.

Wizards became alchemists also, claiming if not actually accomplishing the transformation of base metals into gold, and of impoverished souls into spiritually magnificent beings.

# †he Magic Wand

Magic itself has always had its own technologies, the methods wizards or sorcerers use to achieve their aims. These range all the way from the creation of ephemerides that enable the reading of horoscopes to the making of a magic wand to help implement spells or conjurations. It is entirely possible that such implements are no more than a length of wood containing no special qualities at all. But accounts from different sources suggest that they are imbued with the energy of the wizards themselves and that they act to both focus and magnify their powers.

A possible point of origin for the wand is the staff, which is often cut from a living tree. This act underscores both the wizard's power over nature and a connection with the living energy of the tree itself. Many wizards carry a wand of this kind, and there are several different versions. One of the oldest depictions of a magic wand is found in a tomb painting dating from ancient Egypt that shows a priest holding a small rod over the head of a bull, which he seems to be charming with its power. At the other end of the spectrum is the wand of Hermes, known as the caduceus. Now widely used as the symbol for medical practitioners, it is generally depicted as a short rod around which two serpents entwine, which represents its bearer's power to heal.

Between these two points we have the rod of Moses, which he was able to transform into a snake and back into a rod again. Joseph of Arimathea had a remarkable flowering staff that blossomed when he placed it in the earth on Wearyall Hill near Glastonbury after he had journeyed there with the Holy Grail in his possession.

**Moses**
This medieval painting shows the magic rod or staff of Moses, which became a serpent at his command.

In Celtic mythology, wizards and druids possess wands that can transform one thing into another. The powerful Welsh wizard Gwydion carried a wand that could transform leaves into gold coins and people into pigs and deer. In the early Irish story of Diarmuid and Grainne, a wizard uses his wand to turn a boy into a pig. The famous wand possessed by the witch Circe turned Odysseus's men into pigs when they arrived on her magical island. In each case, the wizard's power is amplified by the possession of a wand.

But this was not the only kind of use to which a wand or rod could be put. As an anonymous seventeenth-century verse proclaims:

> *Some sorcerers do boast they have a rod*
> *Gathered with vows and sacrifices*
> *And (born about) will strangely nod*
> *To hidden treasure where it lies.*

This image suggests the divining rods of later times, which are used for everything from discovering water to locating treasure.

To this day, the figure of the stage magician would not be complete without his wand. In some parts of the world, societies such as the International Brotherhood of Magicians arrange special wand-breaking ceremonies at the funerals of their members, proving that the association of the wizard with his wand of power is far from dead.

**The wand**
Modern magicians continue to use a magic wand in many of their illusions.

*Left:* **Merlin**
Nicol Williamson in the role of Merlin from John Boorman's 1981 movie *Excalibur*.

# Artifacts of Wonder

Another kind of creation attributed to the wizard involves devices that appear to be magical, although they are constructed by human hands. The wizard pope, Gerbert of Aurillac, who as we learned in Chapter 4 was an extremely well-educated man, is also reputed to have erected a marvelous clock in Magdeburg, Germany. It was said to register the motions of the heavens and to record the exact moment when the sun rose and set. The redoubtable historian and traveler William of Malmsbury recorded that Gerbert was also responsible for a wonderful set of hydraulic machines in the city of Rheims. These not only caused water to flow from various fountains but also played music. William also recorded his own visit to an extraordinary underground chamber created by Gerbert's magic that vanished at the slightest touch of a human hand.

Dr. Dee, while teaching classics at Trinity College, Cambridge, produced a performance of Aristophanes' play *Pax*, which involved, among other things, the character Scarabeus flying up to visit the god Jupiter. To achieve this illusion, Dee created a device whose precise nature is still uncertain but that enabled the actor playing the part to fly, complete with a basket of food on his back, into the heavens. "Whereat," Dee remarks in his *True and Faithful Rehearsal,* "was great wondering, and many vain reports spread abroad of the means how this was effected." In all probability this was nothing more than an elaborate piece of machinery, but it may have been the first time such a device had been used on the English stage, and it certainly helped build Dee's reputation as a wonder-worker.

Another, and very different, figure, the philosopher and polymath Athanasius Kircher (1602–1680) ran into similar problems when he constructed a series of moving images for a play attended by the archbishop of Mainz. It was touch-and-go as to whether Kircher would be accused of magic for carrying out this miraculous display. But being less of a showman than Dee, he simply revealed how his engines were constructed. In the end, he earned himself a higher position in the world of the European intelligentsia.

Such demonstrations of skill—which are often dubbed unearthly by those who view them—are an important aspect of the wizards' art. They demonstrate their mastery over the natural world and their ability to summon otherworldly beings to make their projects successful. Through their mastery over stones and other natural materials that are used to make a wand or staff, wizards can channel their power in whatever way they wish. Whether they seek simply to impress an audience or genuinely move mountains with their art, harnessing the power of the elements gives them an edge over those who wish to decry their gifts.

**Artifacts of Wonder**

A design for a mechanical organ built by Athanasius Kircher for the Pope. Pan, god of harmony, and a phoenix are depicted as the magical inspiration of the device.

115

# THE BRAZEN HEAD

**Roger Bacon**
The twelfth-century wizard-monk
Roger Bacon reading from a book
of magical emblems.

Among the most fascinating records we possess of the magical creations of various wizards are those that describe the work of Friar Roger Bacon (c. 1214–1294). In our own time, Bacon is considered one of the founding fathers of modern science. Known as "Doctor Mirabilis," he is credited with the creation of one of the first telescopes and the first pair of eyeglasses, and with the first use of gunpowder in the West. He even wrote about the possibility of powered flight, a dream that was to be taken up by an even more famous explorer of forbidden knowledge, Leonardo da Vinci. Bacon was regarded as at best a madman and at worst a heretic and practitioner of magic. Yet he seems to have gotten away with a great deal more than most wizards of his time and he was able to publish a number of scholarly works that show the depth of his knowledge and the dedication with which he pursued his explorations of science, alchemy, and natural magic.

After his death, various legends sprang up around his name. One described his construction of a head of bronze that, inhabited by a spirit, was able to foretell the future and offer knowledge far outside human understanding:

## THE STORY OF THE BRAZEN HEAD

For many years Friar Bacon pursued his quest for the secrets of magic and alchemy. But one great task always escaped him—the construction of a wall of brass around the shores of Britain, as Merlin was believed to have done in his time, in order to protect the island from invasion. Despite long labors, Bacon could not accomplish this goal, and so he began work on another task: the creation of a speaking head of brass that would foretell all dangers that might arise. But even this proved beyond his skills—until, that is, he met Friar Bungay, a fellow seeker and a great alchemist in his own right. Together, the two men labored long into the night. After several weeks they had constructed the head, which resembled that of a human being in all aspects but refused to speak. They decided to call up a spirit and to command it to cause the head to become animated. So they cast a circle on the earth and uttered many invocations, until at last the spirit stood before them.

"We have created this head of brass," said Bacon, "but we cannot make it speak. Tell us how we can do so or we shall bind you to this earthly sphere forever."

"You shall make a smoke and a fume of six fires that shall be the hottest you can make them," answered the demon. "Place the head within the smoke and leave it for one month. Within that time it shall speak. But be warned—if you fail to hear it when it utters its first words, it shall never speak again."

Friar Bacon and Friar Bungay set to work. They built six great fires and fed them constantly so that the smoke rose from them in dark plumes. In the center of this column of smoke they placed the brazen head. Then they prepared for a long vigil, taking it in turns to watch the head at all times so that one at least would be present when it spoke.

Several days passed and Friar Bungay, worn out with lack of sleep, fell ill. Shortly after that Friar Bacon became so exhausted that he decided to put his servant, a simple fellow named Miles, to oversee the work, while he caught up on sleep. While the two friars slept Miles watched, humming small tunes to himself and telling jokes to the silent head.

Finally, the brazen head opened its metal jaws and spoke. "Time is," it said.

Miles laughed at it and thought his master would not want to be awakened for such a platitude as this.

"Time was," said the head in its metallic voice.

Again Miles laughed, thinking his master would want to hear only words of wisdom from his creation.

A third time the head of brass spoke: "Time is not," it said.

Then, with a great crash, it exploded, waking Friar Bacon, whose anger knew no bounds when he realized that he had failed to hear the first words spoken by the head and had therefore lost the opportunity forever. After that, he never again tried to create a head of brass but looked to other ways of predicting the future.

✦ ✦ ✦ ✦ ✦

This story may well have originated from an Arabic folktale, but the image of a speaking head became powerfully attached in the popular imagination to a number of early scholars who dared to press the bounds of knowledge beyond the limits set by the Church. In the preceding story, the mysterious words uttered by the brazen head suggest that the servant had let his master's chance of consulting the oracle slip by. But they are sometimes taken as an enigmatic comment on the meaning of time and are frequently found inscribed on sundials to this day.

Bacon is typical of the many wizards who set out to show that magic was natural and that, through its use, miraculous artifacts could be constructed to help humankind. Bacon himself believed that if Christianity was to survive, it had to expand its store of knowledge far beyond what was considered appropriate to the time. His beliefs naturally got him into trouble, and though he remained a friar in the order of St. Francis to the end, he was at last imprisoned and almost certainly died in prison. His thinking, like that of other mages of his time and succeeding ages, helped to further the progress of the modern magic of science as well as keep alive the mystery of the ancient past.

# Making a Magical Talisman

T he word *talisman* comes from the Greek *teleo*, meaning "to consecrate." Wizards use magical talismans for many purposes. Essentially, they are intended to act as a magical focus, a memorial to the action required by the magician. Talismans can be used to help obtain better exam results, to improve a love relationship, or for health, as well as many other purposes. Essentially, when you use a talisman you consecrate your intent and the object you create to whatever your need.

Everything to do with the creation and use of an effective magical talisman (as with most magical work) has to do with intent. If such a task is undertaken as a joke, or with no real intent behind it, it is not likely to work. The whole secret of making a talisman revolves around a determined effort, a focusing of the will, and a dedication to the action that impresses itself upon every step of the process, imbuing the talisman with the desired qualities.

Let us suppose that you desire to make a talisman to bring better health for yourself or someone else. First, you need to establish exactly what it is you are seeking to achieve: perhaps better general health or healing for a specific problem or part of the body? If you are creating a talisman for someone, make sure that person is fully in agreement and understands what you are doing.

Next, decide what kind of talisman you are going to make. The most common and effective kind is one that invokes a planetary influence. Such talismans have been in use for hundreds of years and are extremely effective. For health and healing you would invoke Mercury, while for love you would seek the power of the planet Venus and inscribe the paper with the symbol that goes with it. The following table shows some of the planets you can invoke and the reasons you might call on them. (These are simply the most basic correspondences; for further details consult one of the books on talismans listed under Further Reading on pages 140–141.)

Having decided what symbol or power you wish to invoke, take a fresh sheet of paper from a new pad. (This is not essential, but it shows that you are beginning a new piece of work for a specific reason and not connecting it with any previous magical action.) Inscribe the symbol or words of your choice on the paper. Try to do this on the day of the week ruled by the planet. (For example, Wednesday for Mercury, Friday for Venus, and so on, as listed below.) Do this while keeping your desired intent in mind. If necessary, write "I invoke the power of the planetary sphere to bring me better luck at work," or some wording of your own. Now take the sheet of paper and fold it. Seal it with wax and place it in a container—a bag or pouch that you have made is the best, but any object that is personal to you serves as well. Carry the talisman with you at all times. If you are making a talisman for someone else, instruct that person to do the same.

This is only one of the many ways to make a talisman. Importantly, remember that you are creating an object that represents the help you wish to invoke and that you are doing so with all the determination you possess. The talisman focuses your intent and draws upon the power of the magical worlds, elements, and beings appropriate to your need.

| NAME | SYMBOL | PURPOSE | DAY |
|---|---|---|---|
| Sun | ☉ | Strength | Sunday |
| Moon | ☽ | Fertility | Monday |
| Mars | ♂ | Courage | Tuesday |
| Mercury | ☿ | Health | Wednesday |
| Jupiter | ♃ | Business | Thursday |
| Venus | ♀ | Love | Friday |
| Saturn | ♄ | Wisdom | Saturday |

**Galahad**
Galahad receives from a wizard the key to the mysterious Castle of Maidans in this painting by Edwin Austin Abbey.

# 6 | The Wizard as Keeper of Knowledge

# DIVINE DOCTORS AND MODERN MAGES

Let my lamp at midnight hour
Be seen in some high lonely tower;
Where I may oft outwatch the Bear
With Thrice Great Hermes.

JOHN MILTON, *"IL PENSEROSO"*

## RESPONDING TO THE WORLD

We have seen how wizards can embody a way of responding to the world, to life and death, and to the infinite. It is this, surely, as much as anything, that prompts our fascination with such figures. Wizards hold keys to existence itself; they can manipulate the elements and create wonders far beyond anything to which we can aspire but of which we can still dream. Whether they are, like Merlin, seeking visions; or, like Solomon, creating temples and palaces; or, like Dr. Dee and the alchemists, exploring the path of human and spiritual evolution, they reflect the way in which we interpret the universe and imagine our own place within it. As such, they become educators and keepers of knowledge, teaching us how to respond and how to deal with the expanding world around us.

In following the history and evolution of the wizard, it has become clear that it is almost impossible to pigeonhole wizards in any satisfactory way. They elude us with continual changes of shape and action. But though their disguises may have changed through the long ages since they first stepped upon the stage in the skin robe and antlered headdress of the shaman, their aims have remained much the same. Contemporary wizards, of whom large numbers exist, follow essentially the same path as their forebears, although their approaches and many of their techniques have changed. Each still uses symbol-laden ritual and visualization techniques to focus his intention to a point where it becomes actualized. Like alchemists striving to be transported into the inner realms, wizards, both past and present, seek to bring to birth the inner impulse in the outer world. They see themselves as divine doctors attending at the birth of each new era.

That this role is also, to some degree, shared by the mystic, the saint, and the philosopher accounts for the difficulty we experience when we try to assign the wizard to any single heading. Indeed, wizards transcend any label or categorization we attempt to put upon them. Like the shaman-in-civilization with which we began, the function of the magician has become fragmented, held together only by an esoteric philosophy that actually underlies much of Western belief (even though this is not always recognized). To understand why, we need to look more closely at that philosophical underpinning and how it has helped shape the history of the wizard.

# A Universe Reborn

The history of the magician (and of magic) has reflected the history of the world and the many changes in attitude to the work of the spirit that have taken place through the ages. The dawn of philosophy in the classical world had a profound effect on the magical traditions, demystifying the teachings that spoke of the hidden order in the cosmos. Where once a steadfast belief in the gods had underpinned all magical activity, now writers like Plutarch (in the second century B.C.E.) could write of "The Obsolescence of Oracles" and poke fun at gullible worshippers at the ancient shrines. Many philosophers were interested only in the physical makeup of the world, and this led in time to the proto-scientific explorations of alchemy. Those who still pursued the teachings of Hermes Trismegistus sought an inner spirituality that was wholly transcendent. But for philosophy as an abstract discipline to survive, it became necessary to concentrate on the exoteric to the exclusion of all else. And this the early philosophers did, creating in an astonishingly short space of time a wholly new way of looking at the universe.

Of course this did not spell the end of the magical tradition, but it did cause a shift away from an open practice of the occult toward a protective secrecy that has cloaked wizards and their magical activities ever since. It was secrecy of a new kind from that of the older mystery schools that had taught the hidden, inner secrets of the gods. Where these had once been accessible to all, now they were kept more closely secret than ever, simply to preserve them. Those who followed the magical road had to move in a twilight world to survive.

This resulted in a curious state of things: Despite a determination to explore pure intellect, many openly continued as devoted servants of the gods at the same time as they were seeking to dispute them. The great classical philosopher Plato was a mystery school initiate who was attacked several times for revealing secret doctrines in public debate.

# Magic through the Ages

Magic itself was constantly redefined through the ages, whether in religious terms or as protoscience or as philosophy. Each person who took up the fragments of the magically oriented past impressed his or her own synthesis upon it. From the earliest times, magic went from a religious discipline to a philosophy and back again, and it continues to share all of these approaches. The figure of the wizard, as we have seen, changed with it, mutating through several guises until what is presently understood by the name bears little or no relation to its origins.

Strangely, because it was the age when all magical activity was likely to earn the ultimate penalty for those who were found to be practicing it, it is the medieval image that has remained most firmly fixed in our consciousness. The strange figure of the medieval wizard—shambling through the darker pages of history with his robe of stars (a leftover from the Persian magi), his pointed hat, and his thick lenses (a symbol of his proto–scientific attitude)—is still a viable image. Figures like Roger Bacon, rather than Merlin, typify the medieval wizard. He is presented as a scholar, cleric, and seeker. He probably exists in minor orders of the Church (the only way he could obtain the books he needed). He became the real inheritor not just of the magic of a shamanic past but also of the classical traditions and the philosophies of Pythagoras and the Platonists.

**Corpus Hermeticum**
Title page from an early edition of the *Corpus Hermeticum*.

In fact, the medieval magus would have been able to understand very little of the original matter of the mysteries. Few remained in the West who could read the texts or who, for that matter, even knew of their existence. Yet the teachings of Hermes Trismegistus did survive. Fragments continued to filter through until, at the height of the Renaissance, the trickle became a flood.

With the publication of the *Corpus Hermeticum*, at the behest of Cosmo di Medici in 1463, the Western world was once more tentatively in touch with its magical past. The connection was tentative because the Renaissance hermeticists and wizards had only texts, not living traditions, with which to perform their revival. They had to grope painfully toward an understanding of what had once been clearly comprehended and practiced by the initiates of the ancient mysteries by means of translations of translations, pied scripts, and tattered classical references. It was a task of unimaginable difficulty, yet the Renaissance hermeticist was equal to the task in enthusiasm if not in a full comprehension of its complexity.

The form of hermeticism set forth by men like the great Renaissance philosopher and magician Marcilio Ficino really dates from Hellenic Egypt and not, as was generally understood at the time, from the age of the Pharaohs. But this misunderstanding enabled a kind of reconciliation between pre-Christian and post-Christian lore, giving the Renaissance thinkers an excuse to delve deeper. This simple mistake in chronology permitted a new renaissance of magic to blossom and provided the foundation upon which the magical revival of the eighteenth century could build.

**Marcilio Ficino**
Marcilio Ficino was one of the greatest of the Renaissance wizards who held keys to the knowledge of both the medieval and classical ages.

# The Return of the Wizard

In late medieval Europe, the mixture of shamanic spirituality and neoclassical magic produced many factors that brought about the reformation of the wizard's character and role and added to his image as a keeper of knowledge. The adoption of neoclassicism fostered only that part of the Hellenic and Egyptian mysteries that had already been externalized sufficiently to make them acceptable and measurable. Renaissance adepts like Ficino, Bruno, Dee, and Francis Bacon succeeded only partially in reconstructing the sources of their own speculations and in disseminating some of their realizations into their own blend of hermetic magic. Perhaps they were too cautious; but their efforts became the foundation of modern Western esotericism, just as hermeticism became, through them, part of the Renaissance.

Pagan, Christian, and hermetic leftovers bobbed in the same melting pot. It was possible to revise archetypes, long outlawed except as educational paradigms, in the persons of the classical gods. Ficino, who was a Christian priest as well as a natural magician, wrote and sang hymns to Apollo; Bruno couched his philosophical speculations about the origin of the cosmos in dialogues between Jupiter and Mercury.

Finally, the magical tradition became secularized, and at the same time the image of the wizard changed from that of an all-powerful, wise, demon-haunted wonder-worker into that of a protoscientist. The great thinkers and natural magicians of the Renaissance were first and foremost Christian; other options were scarcely open to them. Yet here also were the old traditions of Greece, Egypt, and Persia. Such beliefs could not easily be discounted. And so there began slowly to emerge a new system based on the ancient mysteries but taking place within the framework of the Christian world.

Such beliefs were considered heretical at the time, but those who practiced them saw things differently. To them the deities were spirits of the air—angelic beings created, like humanity, to serve God and creation. Thus, while the older pantheon of gods and goddesses became Christianized to a degree, they lost none of their energy. The figure of the wizard stood at the center of such beliefs and traditions—appearing there fully fledged, like Merlin after a sleep of centuries.

Hermetic texts, kabbalistic translations, and scientific experimentation conjured up new possibilities. Utopian myths were explored by scholar-wizards, such as Francis Bacon (not to be confused with the earlier Roger), each one embodying a perfect world where magic was part of the divine, and where the microcosm reflected the macrocosm as perfectly as possible.

The Renaissance wizard must often have wondered how really close to perdition wizards had been during the intervening centuries when esoteric pursuits of any kind had earned an inevitable stigma. Now their concerns were part of the intellectual world of Europe, to be openly examined, codified, and debated. A new breed of magician entered the scene, one who was recognized as a keeper of divine knowledge and wisdom, whose worldview included the mysteries of the stars and the very nature of creation itself. Not, of course, that this was in any sense new; magicians and wizards had been working with such matters since the beginning of history. What was different was that they now approached their work with the precision and exactitude of the scientist. Of the many leading figures of the Renaissance who pursued the role of magician alongside that of philosopher and scientist, two men in particular embodied this new approach to magic. Despite the fact that they uttered no spells and conjured no demons, their intellectual pursuits earn them a place at the table with the wizards we have discussed.

# The Sage of Nola

Giordano Bruno (1548–1600) was among the most influential thinkers of his time. Born at Nola in the shadow of Mount Vesuvius, he joined the Dominican order at the age of fifteen. However, he was soon expelled on suspicion of heresy and set out on a wandering path across Europe, teaching in Paris, Oxford, and Prague. Though a Christian, his beliefs drew heavily on hermetic philosophy and kabbala. He believed that by implementing the teachings of the hermeticists, especially those believed to originate in Egypt, the world could be restored to a golden age where corruption, war, and disease were banished and the celestial sun burned brightly at the heart of the universe. In a memorable passage from his book *De la Causa, Principio, et Uno*, Bruno distinguished between those who could see the splendor of the spiritual sun and those who preferred to dwell in the darkness of ignorance:

> *Some men, resembling the dim-eyed mole, who the moment he feels upon him the open air of heaven, rushes to hide himself back again into the ground, desire to remain in their native darkness. . . . But those who are born to see the sun, being full of thanksgiving when they come to the end of the loathsome night, dispose themselves to receive in the very center of their eyes' crystal globe their long expected rays of the glorious sun, and with unaccustomed gladness in their hearts, they lift up hands and voices to adore the east.*

Trans. Frances B. Yeats

With opinions like these, it is small wonder that Bruno was consistently persecuted by the church. He was finally arrested by the Inquisition in 1592 and imprisoned for more than eight years. Though he recanted while under duress, he was retried in Rome and this time refused to deny his beliefs. He was burned at the stake as a heretic in 1600 and left behind a number of works that helped to keep the idea of a hermetic revival in the minds of magicians and thinkers across Europe.

**Giordano Bruno**
Statue of Giordano Bruno in Rome, Italy. One of the great masters of Renaissance magical philosophy, he was burned as a heretic in 1600 C.E.

# The Priest and the Sage

A thanasius Kircher (1602–1680), who saw himself as a follower of Bruno, is unusual both for the fact that he was a Jesuit priest and because he promoted a magical view of the universe at a time when his fellow scientists, Newton and Kepler (despite their secret interest in magic), were doing their best to reduce the world to a set of quantifiable rules. As though in response to this narrowing of perception, Kircher seemed bent on expanding his vision of the universe as far as possible. An accomplished musicologist, linguist, and archaeologist, Kircher also made magical toys for nobles and cardinals, invented an entire symbolic language, and studied everything from Egyptian hieroglyphics to kabbala. In addition, though he remained a practicing Catholic, Kircher was every bit as fascinated by the Hermetic writings as Bruno. He simply found ways to explore them without earning the accusation of heresy.

Born at Geisa in Germany, the ninth child of a polymath father, Kircher showed early promise and was schooled in Hebrew by a local rabbi along with his lessons in the nearby Jesuit school. A number of near brushes with death while still in his teens convinced him that he was singled out by God for some great work. After this, his life was a catalogue of extraordinary events, including a remarkable number of further close escapes from death. As the Thirty Years' War raged across Europe, he narrowly escaped Protestant attacks and fled to Cologne. On the way he was captured by Protestant soldiers who were prepared to hang him until one of the soldiers, observing his calm demeanor in the face of death, spoke up for him. Having saved his life, the soldier even gave him some money to continue his journey. Once at Cologne, Kircher began a spectacular career as a philosopher and mathematician. Like John Dee, his skills in arranging a wonderful display of moving scenery and fireworks for a visiting archbishop brought accusations of black magic. But, being less of a showman than Dee, Kircher simply explained the mechanical workings of his artifices and was let off with a caution.

Kircher traveled onward to Speir, where he was ordained as a priest. He applied for a position in China but was not accepted. So he remained in Würzburg, where he studied astronomy and Egyptian hieroglyphics while teaching theology. One night he was awakened by a vision that the college was

**Athanasius Kircher**

Portrait of Athanasius Kircher, age 62, painted in 1664. The enigmatic inscription reads: "Painter and poet say in vain: he's here: his face and fame are known throughout the earth's sphere."

being attacked. No one believed him at first, but shortly thereafter, the buildings were indeed attacked and Kircher, along with several of his fellow Jesuits, narrowly escaped capture.

After this, Kircher decided to leave Germany. He traveled to Italy and settled for a time in Avignon. Then he was summoned to take up the post of mathematician to the Hapsburg court in Vienna. He never reached there, however, because an influential nobleman in Rome wanted Kircher to continue to research the meaning of hieroglyphics. Again proving that he lived a charmed life, he safely arrived in Rome despite being shipwrecked twice, having his goods stolen by pirates, and almost being killed in an eruption of Mount Etna.

Kircher continued to explore the hidden corners of human wisdom, and when he died in 1680 at the age of seventy-eight he was famed throughout the intellectual circles of Europe. His quest for lost and forgotten knowledge had been taken up by secret Hermeticists and practitioners of alchemy, and though it was never his avowed intention, this remarkable man had pushed the borders of esoteric knowledge far beyond anything imaginable before.

# Magic into Science

Bruno and Kircher were by no means alone in their speculative approach to the workings of the world. Robert Flud (1574–1637) combined medicine, alchemy, and hermetic magic in his work, spreading Hermetic wisdom as he traveled the roads of Europe. Paracelsus (a pseudonym adopted by Theophrastus Bombastus von Hohenheim, c. 1493–1541) transformed medicine by introducing alchemy and natural magic into his practice. Thomas Charnock (c. 1524–1581) wrote celebrated poems based on alchemical texts and was friend to both John Dee and Edward Kelly. George Starkey (1627–1666) pursued alchemical studies in New England while earning two degrees at Harvard University. His works were also known to the great New England scientist Benjamin Franklin (1706–1790), who, despite being better known as statesman, was also interested in alchemy and natural magic and saw himself as the inheritor of Freemasonic traditions. Though not a wizard in the true sense, he bore many of the characteristics of a magician and was recently portrayed as such in a wonderful trilogy of novels by J. Gregory Keyes, published under the collective title of *The Age of Unreason*, that present an alternative view of the universe where magic and alchemy are very real.

It is on the shoulders of these men that most of modern theoretical science stands, just as they, in turn, stood upon the shoulders of the medieval and Renaissance wizards and the classical magi—all the way back to the first shamans. Without their intellectual explorations into the often forbidden areas of human knowledge, the world would be a very different place.

**Robert Flud**
Robert Flud combined alchemy, magic, and medicine in his work. He influenced several generations of wizards who followed in his footsteps. Portrait by Matthieu from *Philosophia Sacra*, 1626.

Si tu ...

meam, Iehova ...

Splendentes efficies

tenebras meas.

Pf: 18. 29.

# Modern Mages

The story of the wizard does not end there. Although the rise of science and the Age of Enlightenment tended to banish an interest in magic to the darker corners of history, fascination with the esoteric arts and the realm of natural magic never truly died out. Esoteric societies and occult orders, such as the Fellowship of the Golden Dawn and its various offshoots, drew those who could not be satisfied with an increasingly quantified view of the universe. Seeing themselves as guardians of a lost knowledge and a forgotten wisdom, modern mages like Madame Blavatsky, Aleister Crowley, A. E. Waite, and W. G. Gray have continued to explore the realm of magic in search of greater truths.

The work of the twentieth- and twenty-first-century wizard tends to focus on the consultation of spiritual forces (known as inner-plane work) with the goal of bringing the world back to a place of balance within both historical and human endeavors. In modern magical practice, there are many individual magicians and wizards working alone. However, a more recent trend has been the assembly of small groups of people that come together to undertake a piece of occult or spiritual work under the direction of a magus. The groups then disband and often will not meet or work together again for several years.

**Magical wands**
Magical regalia of the Hermetic Order of the Golden Dawn, one of a number of esoteric societies founded in the nineteenth and twentieth centuries.

One of the most significant of the modern mages, and someone whose life typifies that of many modern magicians, is the British occultist Dion Fortune. She was born Violet Mary Firth in Wales on December 6, 1890. Her father was a solicitor and her mother was a Christian Scientist. The family fortune acquired through steel manufacture and their company's motto *Deo, non Fortuna* (by God, not chance) later became the basis for Violet's magical name. She had visions of Atlantis as a child and later believed that she had lived there as a priestess. In 1906 the family moved to London, where Violet briefly joined the Theosophical Society. However, this group did not offer enough depth to satisfy her and she left it soon after, finding it trivial and unsatisfying for her already burgeoning interest in psychic matters.

In her twenties, Fortune went to work for an educational institution, where she encountered a woman whom she believed was psychically attacking her. Though she managed to rebuff the attacks, she suffered a nervous breakdown in the process and was ill for the next three years. During this time she studied psychology, especially the writings of Carl Jung, and began to form her own ideas concerning the operation of magical forces in the universe. She was a lay psychoanalyst for a brief period and then joined the Land Army when World War I began. As a result, she met an extraordinary Irish magician named Theodore Moriarty, whom she later immortalized in a series of occult tales called *The Secrets of Dr. Taverner* (1926).

Continuing to pursue her studies, Fortune was initiated in 1919 into the London Temple of the Stella Matutina Lodge, an offshoot of the celebrated Hermetic Order of the Golden Dawn. There she encountered leading figures from London's esoteric community, including A. E. Waite, Aleister Crowley, and Samuel MacGreggor Mathers, whose wife, Moina, she later claimed psychically attacked her. Founding her own group, the Fraternity (later Society) of the Inner Light, Fortune split off (or was expelled) from the Golden Dawn. After moving to Glastonbury in 1923, she began a period of intense inner work. Among the inner-plane masters she looked to for resources were the Greek philosopher Socrates; Henry VIII's chancellor, Thomas More; and the famous seventeenth-century French magician, Comte de Saint Germain.

In 1927, Dion Fortune met and married Thomas Penry Evans, a Welsh doctor with occult interests. Their marriage, which was reportedly stormy, lasted twelve years but ended in divorce. After this Dion Fortune began to divide her time between Glastonbury and London. She founded a temple dedicated to the mysteries of Isis and became a well-known figure in the occult circles of the time. Her writings included a number of best-selling novels, as well as a series of books on magic that have yet to be bettered. Her influence on the modern esoteric movement was profound. By reforging the ancient idea of the mysteries and contemporary notions of magic, she restored something that had been separated since the end of the classical era. Her focus on the importance of the feminine principle brought this much-needed presence that had been latent for decades into the sphere of modern magical work. Her work with the native traditions of the Celts, together with the Arthurian legends, restored this dimension of magical awareness to the practice of the modern magus. She also showed how magic could be an utterly contemporary and everyday practice that could add to the quality of life in numerous ways.

After her death in 1946, her mediumistic presence continued to be felt in the Lodge of the Inner Light. This fraternity remains active to this day, offering courses in the Western esoteric tradition. Several generations of modern esotericists, such as Gareth Knight, Dolores Ashcroft-Nowicki, and W. G. Gray, have acknowledged her importance in their own work. Many practicing magicians honor her as a founding mother of modern esoteric practice.

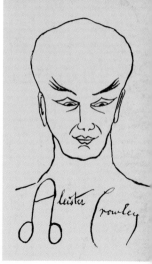

**Aleister Crowley**
Self-portrait by Aleister Crowley, in which he depicts himself with demonic features. Crowley was believed by many to be the most powerful wizard of his age.

# Twentieth-Century Wizards

**J.R.R.Tolkien**
J.R.R.Tolkien, whose opus
*The Lord of the Rings* has done
much to promote the figure of
the wizard in our time.

***The Lord of the Rings***
Sir Ian McKellen as the wizard
Gandalf the Grey in the movie
version of Tolkien's great work.

In more recent years, access to the figure of the wizard has been largely through the domain of fiction. The most famous modern wizards are to be found in the works of writers such as T. H.White, J. R. R. Tolkien and J. K. Rowling. White's portrait of Merlyn (his spelling) in the best-selling *The Once and Future King* draws upon the traditions of the great Arthurian magus. A distinctly twentieth-century gloss is added through his fate of living backward so that he has already seen the future and grows younger as the years progress.

Tolkien (1892–1973) was an Oxford don whose astonishing work lay in the creation of an entire world. Middle Earth was peopled with a vast collection of characters and races. The literary history of the wizard was taken to new heights with the creation of Gandalf the Grey. He is one of five "Istari," immortal spirits whose role it is to watch over the world and hold in check the power of evil. He appears in the traditional guise of wizards: White-bearded, with pointed hat, cloak, and staff. Gandalf is primarily involved in the discovery of a magical token, the evil One Ring that has the power to enslave the free peoples of the world. Gandalf finds this ring in the keeping of a simple Hobbit, one of a race of small, woolly footed folk living in a forgotten corner of the world. He then fulfills one of the chief roles of the wizard by acting as a guide to the nine beings selected to destroy the Ring and as a power behind the throne once the true kings of Middle Earth are safe from the power of the Ring and its evil creator.

There are other notable wizards featured in *The Lord of the Rings*. They include Radagast the Brown, who is perhaps closer to the shaman aspect of the wizard because his concern is primarily the animals and birds of Middle Earth. The complex Saruman is called "the Man of Skill." His thirst for knowledge finally draws him to seek the power of the Ring for himself, which leads him down a path of darkness and petty evil. Tolkien draws upon the entire history of wizards for the creation of these characters, who possess shamanistic, political, magical, and spiritual powers.

Tolkien's books have sold millions of copies all over the world. His work spawned countless imitators, few of whom have ever reached his heights of creativity. Ursula le Guin's *Earthsea* quartet, however, has created an unforgettable portrait of a wizard in the shape of her hero, Ged, an apprentice who struggles against his

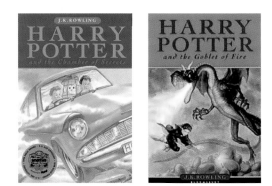

**Harry Potter**
The success of J. K. Rowling's series of books featuring the young wizard Harry Potter (portrayed here by Daniel Radcliff in the movie version) shows a continuing interest in all things magical.

own inner conflicts to become a great practitioner of the magical arts. Other contemporary authors—such as Terry Goodkind, Robert Jordan, and Katherine Kurtz—have all added significant wizard figures to the ranks of the traditional models.

But the latest and most notable representative of the wizard is undoubtedly Harry Potter, hero of a phenomenally successful series of books by British author J. K. Rowling. Since the appearance of the first book in the ongoing series, *Harry Potter and the Philosopher's Stone* (renamed *Harry Potter and the Sorcerer's Stone* in the United States), a huge amount of interest in magic and magicians has been generated. Harry, a nine-year-old boy when the series opens, has inherited the skills and abilities of his parents, who were wizards killed by the evil Voldemort. He is gradually introduced into a kind of parallel world in which magic is the accepted norm by attending the famous Hogwarts Academy for Wizards and Witches. The magic of the Harry Potter books is generally humorous stuff, written with its young audience in mind. But it is based on a long tradition of wizards. Thus, we hear of Nicholas Flamel, who created the philosopher's stone and was able through its magic to sustain his life far beyond the span of ordinary men. Flamell was, of course, an alchemist whose work on the fashioning of the stone follows fairly closely that described by J. K. Rowling. Dr. Albus Dumbledore, the venerable headmaster of Hogwarts, also bears a striking resemblance to the popular conception of Merlin, while the other wizardly characters run the whole gamut from Dr. Dee to Rasputin.

# THE FUTURE OF MAGIC

Our search for the wizard has led us to a number of realizations, many of which have to do with the part we ourselves play in the continuing history of the cosmos. Virtually every wizard we have discussed here can trace his magical lineage back to the teachings of Hermes and the Emerald Tablet. They continue to tell us that things change, that the universe is growing, and that we are a part of that change and growth.

Nowhere within a contemporary framework is this better stated than in the world of *Star Wars*. The mystical Force that dominates so much of the magical action within the movies and books represents one of the clearest restatements of an ancient idea threading the life and deeds of the wizard. The Force is part of the natural order of things and manifests in those who learn how to sense it and allow it to flow though them. They, in turn, learn to master their own inner forces and to manipulate the world around them. In the movie *The Empire Strikes Back*, the Jedi master Yoda says to his apprentice Luke Skywalker: "You must feel the force around you. Here, between you . . . me . . . the tree . . . the rock . . . everywhere!" This could stand as a clear statement of the nature of the wizard's power, which comes not from himself but from a harmonious relationship with nature. For us, as for the characters of the *Star Wars* universe, the wizard can be seen to represent the best of human endeavor.

It is this kind of attainment that the wizard of the future must seek if he or she is to survive in a changing and expanding universe. Few writers have yet managed to create a character who embodies such precepts. Possibly, however, Michael J. Straczynski came near to it in his TV series *Babylon 5* and *Crusade*. Here the beings known as the Techno-Mages are introduced as those who have successfully married magic and science to the point where one appears to be the same as the other. This is very close to what the magicians of the Renaissance were seeking when they set out to bring together the philosophy and precepts of the ancient mystery religions, the wonder-working abilities of their medieval ancestors, and their own realization of the way the universe works.

**Star Wars**
George Lucas's futuristic myth *Star Wars* presents the aspects of the wizard's story in a fresh, new way.

# The Legacy of Magic

No magician, either in the past or the present, could progress very far in his search for knowledge without recognizing the unity of all things. The use of magic itself is a tacit acknowledgment that the individual is connected intimately with the whole universe of time and space. The signature recognizable in everything, by whatever name it is known, makes all matter interactive, in turn promoting the understanding that whatever is done has repercussions for the rest of creation.

Magic is not an exact science. The effects of working magically are subjective, as in any art. Yet magic, like the science of engineering, can be used to build bridges and convey loads. The magician is himself a bridge between higher and lower realms, between the divine and the mundane. He works constantly within the framework of the first great precept of the Emerald Tablet, that "everything that is above is as everything that is below, and everything that is below is as everything that is above."

It is in this belief that the wizard constantly places himself as close to the heart of creation as he can in order to work from and with it, absorbing both the differences and the similarities that are present everywhere. Seeking to realize his potential within the framework of matter, he becomes a visionary, an artificer, and a keeper of knowledge. As the modern-day philosopher and educator David Spangler wisely noted: "The wizard is someone who hollows himself out so that he can be filled with the potential of the cosmos."

Magic can be seen as a higher understanding of nature, a true vision of the universe as it whirls and roars around us. From the rituals of the ancient shamans to the high magic of the Renaissance magician and the work of the modern occult revival, this has been the heart and center of the wizard's life. Wizards' work has almost always arisen out of a fundamental belief in an ordered cosmos of which we are all a part. As such, they have much to teach us, even in today's technological universe. Figures such as Merlin and John Dee, Giordano Bruno and Athanasius Kircher helped to build the world in which we live and, if still living, would undoubtedly be at the forefront of our attempts to create a new and better future.

The wizard remains a vital figure in the landscape of our dreams, embodying many of our hopes for a world where magic continues to reign in the heart and soul, teaching us to understand more fully than ever our own part in its unfolding mystery.

*The Astrologer*
Painting by N. C. Wyeth from *Tales* by Mark Twain.

# Meeting Dr. Dee

ohn Dee is one of the most important figures in the history of the wizard, not only because he exercised considerable power in the outer world but also because he brings together so many of the characteristics we have been studying. Dee is at once seer, artificer, alchemist, keeper of knowledge, and seeker of wisdom from the angelic realms. Who better, even now at the beginning of the twenty-first century, than this great Elizabethan magus to give us the gift of understanding and wisdom (if we choose to take it), to end this brief course of studies in the training of the wizard and, perhaps, to point the way forward?

Many wizards have testified that they were taught by beings who had no physical reality or who chose to hide it. Access to inner knowledge—the source of much of the wizard's power—is always possible if approached with the right frame of mind. The following visualization is intended to offer an opportunity to learn and to grow, which has been the aim of all wizards from the beginning of time. How you choose to react to it is for you alone to decide. So, following the instructions for the meditation at the end of Chapter 1, settle down and begin your greatest journey into the world of the wizard.

Once again see before you the great door that is studded with nails. Its handle is in the form of the lion-headed man with a ring in his mouth. When you push the door, it opens at once, admitting you to the familiar wood-paneled room with the fire burning brightly on the hearth. This time, however, you are aware at once of a figure seated at the table, who rises to his feet as you enter. You recognize at once the face of Dr. John Dee, alchemist to Queen Elizabeth I and the greatest wizard of his time. He holds out his hand and you take it, aware that he is scrutinizing you deeply. Now he invites you to be seated in a chair by the fire and he seats himself so that you are facing each other. Dr. Dee holds out his hands toward the flames and, looking keenly at you, asks you to describe your studies as an apprentice wizard. . . . You tell him how you have progressed through the practices outlined in this book. . . . Dr. Dee then asks if you wish to continue your studies. . . . This is an important question, an opportunity for you to state before this witness your intention. Take as long as you need, and if you have any hesitations or questions put them to your companion. . . .

When you have spoken about this, Dr. Dee rises and crosses to the table. He chooses a small wooden box, intricately carved with signs and symbols of the wizard's trade. This he hands to you with these words: "Within this box is a great gift: the gift of knowledge. Think carefully before you open it, and consider deeply what is implied. Once you open this box you will be changed. Knowledge will come to you, not necessarily at once but over the months that follow. It is the first step on the path that is the wizard's way."

Taking the box, you sit for a time with it in your lap, considering the doctor's words and your response to them. Will you open the box and receive the gift of wisdom, or will you decide to put it aside for the moment? Remember that you can do this journey again at any time and that the same gift will be offered then. It is no dishonor to refuse the offer, for not everyone is ready to take up such a great task. . . .

Whatever you decide makes no difference to what happens next. Thank Dr. Dee for the offer of the knowledge of wizards. Whether or not you chose to

open the box, now the doctor has another gift for you. He rises again and from a place by the fire, where it has been leaning, takes a staff. Tall and gnarled, it radiates energy that you can clearly feel. Dr. Dee holds it out to you.

"Every wizard must have a staff," he says. "You have proved yourself to be an apt pupil in the work you have undertaken. Therefore I give this to you with my blessing. Carry it with honor and be certain never to misuse its power. A wizard's staff is an extension of you and a powerful companion in your journeys throughout the worlds. Wherever you go, in this world or the other, be aware of the staff. Take it with you at all times, for it will stand you in good stead when you have need of strength and fortitude. Go now with my blessing."

The great doctor stands for a moment, and as you take the staff you both briefly hold it before Dr. Dee releases his grasp. In that moment a surge of energy passes between you. Then it is gone, and slowly now the scene begins to fade. You are back in your normal surroundings, but you remain aware of the wizard's staff that has been given to you. You also clearly perceive the box with the knowledge of wizards, whether you chose to open it in this visualization or to

postpone that moment until you feel ready. Remember that you can return to the wizard's room whenever you wish and explore it. You may indeed find other things there in the future, as well as meet other great wizards from the past and the present. One may even choose to become your teacher. The outcome rests with you, but the access to this inner training is always available should you wish to seek it out.

You too can become a wizard.

# Further Reading

Ashe, Geoffrey. *The Book of Prophecy*. London, Blandford, 1999.

Becker, Udo. *The Element Encyclopedia of Symbols*. Shaftsbury, Dorset, Element Books, 1984.

Buddle, Thomas. *The Aborigines of New Zealand*. Auckland, 1851.

Butler, E. M. *The Myth of the Magus*. London, Cambridge University Press, 1979.

Christian, P. *The History and Practice of White Magic*. London, Forge Press, 1952.

Ficino, Marsilio. *The Book of Life*. Trans. Charles Boer. Irving, TX, Spring Publications, 1980.

Fortune, Dion. *Psychic Self-Defence*. Wellingborough, Aquarian Press, 1976.

French, Peter J. *John Dee*. London, Routledge, Keegan Paul, 1972.

Godwin, Joscelyn. *Kircher*. London, Thames and Hudson, 1979.

Goodkind, Terry. *Wizard's First Rule*. London, Millennium, 1994.

Hall, Manley P. *Sages and Seers*. Los Angeles, Philosophical Research Society, 1959.

Hauck, Dennis William. *The Emerald Tablet*. London, Penguin Arkana, 1999.

Kurtz, Katherine, and Deborah Turner Harris. *The Adept Series*. New York, Ace Books, 1991.

LeGuin, Ursula. *The Earthsea Quartet*. London, Penguin Books, 1993

Lonnrot, Elias. *The Kalevala*. Trans. Francis Peabody Magoun. Cambridge, MA, and London, Harvard University Press, 1963.

Loomis, C. Grant. *White Magic*. Cambridge, MA, The Medieval Academy of America, 1948.

McLeish, Kenneth. *Stories and Legends from the Bible*. London, Longman, 1998.

Marshall, Peter. *The Philosopher's Stone*. London, Macmillan, 2001.

Matthews, Caitlín and John. *The Encyclopedia of Celtic Wisdom*. London, Rider, 2001.

Matthews, John & Caitlín. *The Encyclopedia of Celtic Myth and Legend*. Rider, 2003.

Matthews, John & Caitlín. *The Western Way*. London, Penguin Arkana, 1994 (Reprinted Inner Traditions, 2003).

Regardie, Israel. *How to Make and Use Talismans*. Wellingborough, Aquarian Press, 1981.

Roberts, Henry C. *The Complete Prophecies of Nostradamus*. New York, American Book, Stratford Press, 1969.

Rowling, J. K. *Harry Potter and the Philosopher's Stone*. London, Bloomsbury Children's Books, 1997.

Sansweet, Stephen J. *Star Wars Encyclopedia*. London, Virgin Publishing, 1998.

Scholem, G. *On the Kabbalah and Its Symbolism*. New York, Schocken Books, 1965.

Shakespeare, William. *Complete Works*. London, The Folio Society, 1997.

Shawn, B. L. *The Legend of the Golem*. New York, 1985.

Sherman, Josepha. *Merlin's Kin: World Tales of the Heroic Magician*. Little Rock, August House, AK, 1998.

Skeleton, Robin. *Talismanic Magic*. York Beech, ME, Samuel Weiser, 1985.

Sutherland, Elizabeth. *Ravens and Black Rain*. London, Constable, 1985.

Thorndike, Lynn. *Michael Scot*. London, Nelson, 1965.

Tolkien, J. R. R. *The Lord of the Rings*. London, Harper Collins, 1991.

White, T. H. *The Once and Future King*. London, Collins, 1952.

**WEBSITE**
For information on courses and books by John and Caitlín Matthews, visit *Hallowquest.org.uk*.

# Index